THE POWER PLAYBOOK

ALSO BY LA LA ANTHONY

The Love Playbook

THE
POWER
PLAYBOOK

RULES FOR INDEPENDENCE, MONEY, AND SUCCESS

LA LA ANTHONY

A CELEBRA BOOK

Celebra
Published by the Penguin Group
Penguin Group (USA) LLC, 375 Hudson Street,
New York, New York 10014

USA / Canada / UK / Ireland / Australia / New Zealand /
India / South Africa / China
penguin.com
A Penguin Random House Company

First published by Celebra,
a division of Penguin Group (USA) LLC

First Printing, May 2015

LIBRARY OF CONGRESS HAS CATALOGING-IN-PUBLICATION DATA:
Anthony, La La.
p. cm.
ISBN 978-0-451-47346-2 (hardback)
1. Success. 2. Success in business. 3. Self-realization in women. I. Title.
BF637.S8A546   2015
650.1—dc23   2015002475

Printed in the United States of America
10 9 8 7 6 5 4 3 2 1

Set in Adobe Garamond
Designed by Spring Hoteling

To Kiyan . . . my heart beats for you.

CONTENTS

Contents

Contents

What Is Power?

*Power is like being a lady . . . If you have to tell
people you are, you aren't.*

—Margaret Thatcher

Character is a power.

—Booker T. Washington

I got my first taste of power pretty early in my career. I was
sixteen years old and working at WHTA in Atlanta as an
intern. Local artists would often show up to the station,
desperate to have their music played on the air. Atlanta
was becoming a hotbed for music, particularly rap and
hip-hop, and our station was the number one station in
town.

Working as the intern for and eventually the assistant

to the music director, Chaka Zulu, I got to see the parade of people who would come through—artists, producers, record labels—all vying for his attention, all in hopes of gaining some opportunity, some introduction, some advantage. They would send over all kinds of gifts just to get that record played.

Chaka held the keys to their success. He had the power. If he decided to put a record into the rotation, it could mean the difference for that artist or record. Eventually, some of that power trickled down to me. Artists started coming to me, too. They knew I had Chaka's ear. He trusted my opinion. I learned that I could have power, even in my lowly position as an intern or assistant, if I could be trusted.

I didn't go to Chaka often with a new artist's tape—in fact, I did it very rarely—so that when I did do it, he was interested in what I had to say.

If I went to him every week or every other day with a tape saying, "This record is hot!" at some point I would lose my power. But if I went once a month, it had more weight.

I also knew that if I told him someone was hot, they had better be hot. If I gave him a tape or CD of an artist and told him they were good and they ended up being whack, he would never trust my opinion again. But if I told him someone was good and they were really good, my word would be valued from then on. And that's what happened. I saw firsthand the power of building my credibility.

I also learned about abuse of power during my first few years in radio. There was something called payola that was very prevalent during this time. Record labels and even artists would pay deejays and program directors to play their songs. Pay for play they called it and it was illegal. I learned that with power comes responsibility and I watched people in the industry get into a lot of trouble because they abused their power or used it in ways that splintered the trust you should have between you and your audience.

Thankfully, we never had any payola at my station, but I paid attention to everything going on in the industry and I remember thinking to myself, "I will never put myself in a position to lose it all over money."

But many people did. They lost their power—and careers—by abusing it. I was just realizing that I could actually have a career in radio—not just a hobby or a love, but I could make a real living. I wasn't about to do anything to jeopardize that.

I got to see the power of being on the radio really play out when I started working in the number two market in the country—Los Angeles. Instead of local artists coming to the station trying to be heard, we saw some of the biggest artists in the business coming through. Record labels were now calling us to see if we'd have on Aaliyah, Method

Man, and Brandy, who were the big names during this time.

"Wow, they are calling *me* to come to *my* show!" It was flattering and exciting, and a little intimidating at first. If I cosigned, or endorsed that artist and his or her music, everyone would think it was cool! That's when I really got a taste of power. I could literally make or break an artist or an album with my opinion on the air.

While I never let it get to my head, I did think it was kind of cool. People were going out of their way to impress me because they wanted me to support their music on the air. I had the power of that mic.

The other side of that was I never knew who was being nice to me because they wanted something. I started thinking everyone had an angle. Do people really like me or are they trying to gain favor for another purpose? Back then radio deejays held all of the cards, and had so much power.

That was my first experience with really having power and it was bittersweet. But it taught me three valuable lessons.

1. Power must be put in perspective.

People will try to use you; they will give you things, do things for you to get your attention and favor. So you have to know who you are first, or else that power can go to your head and you will think it's all about you when it's really only about what you can do for someone else.

2. Power should never be abused.

Just because you have the power to help someone, you should never use that power to hurt or control another. If you use your power for anything other than doing the right thing, it can have bad results. I heard about people losing their livelihoods and careers and even ending up in jail over payola, a prevalent abuse of power in music. It wasn't worth it.

3. Embrace power in moderation.

I liked the way I felt when I could control my own destiny, when I had the connections to make the calls and get the meetings I wanted, and even when I had the power to help others. Power is contagious. The more you have, oftentimes the more you want. But for me, it was always about having the power to do things for others and myself. I wanted to be able to open doors, to make paths smoother and easier for my friends and family. I liked how that felt and I wanted to be able to do that on an even larger scale. What I knew for sure was that I never wanted to be powerless.

Everyone I know seems to have read *The 48 Laws of Power* by Robert Greene. It is this generation's version of *The*

Prince by Machiavelli or *The Art of War* by Sun Tzu. This book is like a bible in the hip-hop community because it lays out how to obtain power in this world.

The book looks at power from the perspective of conquering countries and conquering people. Greene acknowledges in the first pages of his book that everyone wants more power, but he warns that it is dangerous to seem too power hungry. So his book illustrates through historical examples how to make power moves being "subtle—congenial yet cunning, democratic, yet devious."

There are laws such as, Law 2: "Never Put Too Much Trust in Friends, Learn How to Use Enemies," Law 7: "Get Others to Do the Work for You, but Always Take the Credit," Law 27: "Play on People's Need to Believe to Create a Cultlike Following," and Law 38: "Think As You Like, but Behave Like Others," that show you how to gain power and how to get ahead.

I believe these laws totally work when you think about the steps it takes to be a political leader or how you work your way up the corporate ladder or how to dominate and conquer an industry like the music or television industry.

I cannot dispute that throughout history men and women have used such rules and laws to gain power.

But for me, the real power starts with control and mastery over yourself—not anyone else.

You can't find success on your own terms unless you first attempt to execute your vision for yourself on your own. No two paths are exactly the same. What works for a friend or a colleague in navigating a tricky situation in the office or in setting up your own business may not be right for you. Only through forging your own way do you find both yourself and your purpose. You can use books like *The 48 Laws of Power* and even my books as guidelines, but you must figure out the path you need to take to be successful.

The process of figuring it out yourself is in and of itself powerful. It's like working a muscle. The more you work it, the more you break it down, the stronger it gets.

Whether you want to be president of your own company or president of the United States, it all starts with you and figuring out who you are and what you really want in life.

That's where I had to start—figuring out what I really wanted and going through life with purpose instead of just letting things happen around me.

Over the last few years I embarked on a career change, launched a new business, created new brands, and wrote a bestselling book. I have traveled all over the world, met a whole bunch of new people, and been introduced to new ideas and opportunities. And as I continue to grow in my craft and in my personal life, I'm learning the value of having power—not necessarily over any particular person or situation, but rather power over myself, and my life. I have learned and put into practice certain rules and laws that have led me to succeed, and I wanted to put those experiences in a book to share with the world.

I can't tell you how often people stop me on the street or hit me up on Twitter or Instagram asking for advice. It started with advice about relationships, which led me to write *The Love Playbook*. The advice has evolved into other areas and I'm getting asked questions like, "I'm in a career I absolutely hate and I'm miserable, what should I do?" and "How do I brand myself?" and "What should I wear on my job interview?"

These are important questions, and while all of our professional paths are different, I certainly have learned a thing or two about getting ahead and finding a career that I love. In this book, I'm sharing my experiences, what I've learned through going out there and doing it the hard way, and what I've learned through watching and listening to others. We're all looking for success in our lives, no matter what that means individually.

And I wanted to explore this thing called power because I believe it's at the root of success. Power can mean a lot of things and, to me, real power starts with a mastery over yourself. So, I set out to develop the best ways for people to find power in their own lives, based on my experiences and those of my friends and family.

I don't know a single person who doesn't want power.

But many people have no clue what true power is, how to get it, and what to do with it when it is obtained. For many, especially women, the idea of wielding power is scary. Many have a twisted idea of what power really is.

For me, it's simple. Power is putting yourself in a position to maximize your gifts and your purpose and execute your goals and plans. Power is something developed from within. It's not about trying to control anyone but yourself.

Power is the strength to face the things you may be afraid to do and then doing them anyway. Power is no regrets. Power is pushing forward. Power is making the tough choices in your life, and even if you fall or fail, having power allows you to get back up and try again.

CHAPTER ONE

The Rules of Engagement

You have to learn the rules of the game. And then
you have to play better than anyone else.

—Albert Einstein

I look at life sometimes as one big game. In a game you need to know the rules to even compete. Can you imagine sitting down at a board game, like Monopoly or chess, and just playing without knowing the rules? You may win eventually, after losing a whole lot and figuring it out. But how much more equipped would you be if you took a moment and studied the rules?

During my career, I have jumped into the game several times without fully understanding the rules and have figured things out. I have also taken time and studied— through watching others and asking questions—and here are some rules I've learned that I believe are the keys to gaining real power—in life and in business.

Rule No. 1: Put Yourself First.

Rule No. 2: Find Your Passion and Your Purpose.

Rule No. 3: Do the Work!

Rule No. 4: Know Your Worth.

Rule No. 5: Be Gracious and Grateful.

Rule No. 1: Put Yourself First.

Everyone knows that my family comes first. My entire life has been about making sure that everyone I love is okay and taken care of. I've always put my son, my husband, my mother, my father, my brother, my grandmother, my cousins, my aunts, and even my close friends, first.

As I've grown older, I've realize that most of my life I have been out of order. I'm realizing how important it is to put myself first. To love me first. It's not selfish to do that, but rather common sense. As much as I worry about everyone in my life, if I'm not okay, then I can't be there to help anyone. All of the pleasure and peace I get from taking care of others will mean nothing if I'm depressed or sad, or I've worked myself so hard that my health fails.

I've always been about making everyone else happy

and that was the source of my happiness. But I'm learning that it's no longer enough. I have to be happy first.

Last year, I launched a new line in my cosmetics business, I was shooting another season of my reality show, *Full Court Life*; I auditioned for two major films; I was starring in a hit television show, which was picked up for another season with my role expanded; I starred in and was on tour promoting *Think Like a Man Too*; and I wrote and went on tour promoting my first book, *The Love Playbook*.

I was doing all of the things I loved and wanted to do—and more. I embraced new opportunities and said yes to exciting new projects. But I found myself exhausted and not sleeping well. I was working so much I would get maybe two hours of sleep a night. I had a moment when I felt so bad I got scared. I finally had to have one of those talks with myself.

You're going to end up in the hospital if you don't slow down!

I have seen it happen—especially in the entertainment business—where people are hustling so hard that they forget to take care of themselves. They are so driven that they ignore when they're tired, they don't eat well, don't exercise, and end up in the hospital with exhaustion. It's real.

What would happen to Kiyan if something happened to me? What would happen to my family? I knew I not only needed balance in my life (which I will talk about later in this book). I also needed to change my priorities in my life, putting health and balance much higher. As much as I love everyone in my life, I have to love myself first and best.

If you don't put yourself first, you cannot build a solid foundation for your life.

Rule No. 2:
Find Your Passion and Your Purpose.

My passion and my purpose are connected but very different. I knew my passion at a very young age. I always knew I wanted to work in the entertainment field. It started with the desire to be on the radio and then it evolved into being on television and now it's evolved again to include acting in television and film. All of this fits under the "entertainment" umbrella.

I know this is my passion because when I'm doing it, I feel fulfilled. It doesn't feel like work. It feels like something I was meant to do and it's rewarding.

I wake up each day thinking about what new adventure I will tackle, what show I will audition for, what movie or television opportunity will come my way. I'm excited about my work. I'm happy when I'm working.

The majority of people I know wake up and go to a job day in and day out, and they're not necessarily happy there.

It's just another day at work. They spend twenty to thirty years of their lives working at a job, which is just a job.

I know how blessed I am to have found my passion at a young age and I have continued to raise the bar and challenge myself and love every minute of it. I know this is my passion because after all of these years I still have the drive. I still care and I want to excel. I'm sad when I'm *not* doing it.

My purpose, which I started realizing about five years ago, is to take care of people. Whether it's my family and friends or my fans through giving advice in person, online, or in my books, I have a desire to help people and see them succeed. I've always been that go-to person who people come to when they want a shoulder to lean on or a word of insight or encouragement.

I can't tell you how many times I've met someone for the first time, struck up a conversation, and had them tell me, "I feel like I've known you all of my life," or "I can't believe I'm telling you this. I've never shared this with anybody," or "You're so easy to talk to, I feel like I can tell you anything."

And they can. Remember my motto: No judgment. That ability to listen to people and not judge them no matter what is my gift. My purpose is to use that gift to help people overcome obstacles in their lives or accomplish things they never thought they could. This book is an extension of my purpose. Instead of telling one person some of the things I've been through and some of the insights that have helped me accomplish things in my life, I can put it all here.

My passion helps me execute my purpose.

Rule No. 3: Do the Work!

I'm married to one of the best basketball players on the planet. He is naturally incredibly athletic and has been specifically talented at basketball since before he can remember. He won an NCAA championship his first year at Syracuse University, the first ever in the team's history. He then left school at just nineteen years old for the 2003 NBA draft, where he was the number three pick.

Basketball comes naturally to him and he probably doesn't have to work as hard as most. But he does. The summer of 2014, after he signed the biggest contract of his career to return to the New York Knicks, he worked harder to prepare for the coming season than I ever saw him work.

He changed his diet—eating low carbs to lose weight so that he would be leaner and faster on the court. And he put in hours-long training sessions twice a day—before training camp was even to begin.

"Babe, aren't you going to have to work this hard for training camp? Why do it now?" I asked him.

"I don't want to be exhausted when training camp gets

here. I want to be in such great shape that it will feel like a breeze," he told me.

He wanted to make sure that he was ready because more than wanting to be the best, he wants to win. When his team isn't winning, he's not a happy camper, no matter how good his personal stats are. He takes it very personally. So he wanted to make sure that he was doing everything in his power to see them victorious.

"This is my team and I have to perform as hard, if not harder, than every man on the team," he told me.

As a team leader, he feels like he has to set the tone. He has to create the standard on his team. And it starts with putting in the work. If his teammates see him putting in the extra time, staying later for practice and working harder than everyone else, it will rub off.

It's not enough to be talented. There are a lot of talented people in the world. But the power move comes in figuring out how to take that talent and do everything in your power to achieve that level of success that you see for yourself.

There may be people who won't hire you for a particular job. In entertainment there is so much rejection. I get rejected at least once a week for a role. But what do I do about it? I work harder. While the reason why I didn't get the job may be outside of my control, I want to make sure that everything that is within my control—my skills, my look, my attitude—I'm working to perfect.

Throughout this book I will give several personal examples of how hard work trumps everything. But I'm most reminded of this quote from Will Smith, to which I totally relate: "I've viewed myself as slightly above average in talent. And where I excel is ridiculous, sickening work ethic."

Rule No. 4: Know Your Worth.

How do you determine your value? For others to know your value, you first have to know your worth. Most of us base our value on what other people think about us or what we've been told our whole life. Only you know your true value. It's based on what kind of person you know you are, what your talents are, and what's the going market for those talents and gifts.

Only you know what you can bring to the table. Only you know your work ethic. Your worth is deeper than salary, though it's easy to fall into the trap of valuing yourself by your paycheck. You are so much more than your job and amount of money you bring home. But I get it; it can be one way to quantify your worth professionally. There is an open market and you can do research on what your salary should be or what people in your field make. But always remember, your worth is deeper than salary.

When I was younger I used to care so much what people thought about me. I wanted everyone to love me. I wanted to reach out to everyone who said something negative about me and let him or her know how cool I was and how wrong they were.

But as I grew up, I cared less and less. Today it doesn't bother me at all. I know who I am and what I have to offer, and no one can take that away from me or detract from it. I will even make a joke out of comments made about me. You can look like Halle Berry and there will be thirty comments on your Instagram page about how messed up you look. That's just people today. If you're going to be upset, you shouldn't be on social media. I'm immune to it now.

Going back to Rule, I had to love myself enough to realize that who I am and what I can accomplish have everything to do with what I put into it. I power my life. I don't give away my power to others to rule my life. I don't need the validation of other people for me to feel good about myself or to assess what I have to offer the world.

There wasn't one moment or one event that happened when I came to realize this. There was a series of events and each time something happened that I thought was devastating and I overcame it, I grew stronger and stronger.

Becoming a mother to my beautiful son Kiyan was a big turning point. There is nothing anyone can say to me or about me that will diminish who I am because I have a son who loves me to my core and as long as that's the case, I'm good. I have a family who loves me. I don't need any outside validation. My worth and value are stored in the knowledge that I am loved.

I am enough.

If you don't feel this way, I suggest you repeat this to yourself every day. Perhaps it's the first thing you do when you wake up. Or, you can try saying it frequently throughout the day like a mantra. Maybe it's a prayer. Maybe you just meditate on that phrase. Whatever you need to do, until you arrive at the place where you know in your heart that you are enough, that you are special, that you have value, you will not have power.

Rule No. 5: Be Gracious and Grateful.

In an industry that's not necessarily known for its kindness and polite behavior, I've seen firsthand the power of simple acts of kindness and courtesy. I have had the pleasure of working with Kevin Hart on a couple of movies now and he is one of the most gracious people I know. During the press junket for *Think Like a Man Too*, the entire cast was all over the country promoting the film. I was paired with Kevin and Terrence J and no matter what city we were in, Kevin would be the first one in the lobby of whatever hotel we were staying in, ready to go with the biggest smile on his face.

I always pride myself on being on time. Punctuality means everything to me. But whenever I arrived, which was usually early, Kevin Hart would already be there waiting with a warm, "How was your evening!" for everyone. Not only was he pleasant, but he was also asking people if they needed anything.

Kevin Hart is arguably one of the most talented comedians of our time. He's definitely a superstar in film but none of that matches his graciousness. It's probably why he works so much.

I learned early in my career that more than talent, people hire people they like being around. You spend a lot of time on a movie set with people. Who wants to be around someone who is unpleasant to be around?

Of course people want to work with talented people or people who are capable. But I can't tell you how much I hear, "If I'm going to be on location for three months I want to be around people I like!"

You might be the best talent for the job, but if your attitude is wrong, the person who may be a lesser talent but a greater person will get the job.

This rule is so important to me that I'm devoting an entire chapter to being gracious, grateful, and nice. It is the true secret of my success and one of the elements that gives me the most power—particularly in my career.

Being nice doesn't take a whole lot of time, and it costs you nothing. It can be the bridge that takes you so much farther than you can ever imagine.

CHAPTER TWO

The Playbook: What's Your Plan?

He who fails to plan, plans to fail.

—Proverb

Without leaps of imagination, or dreaming, we lose the excitement of possibilities. Dreaming, after all, is a form of planning.

—Gloria Steinem

I didn't really start planning my career until after I had my son, Kiyan. Before this, I was pretty much on autopilot, taking one opportunity as it came. Sure, I had dreams and goals, and I actively pursued opportunities. But it was mostly just moving up the ladder, taking better positions as the opportunities presented themselves. I never actually sat down and came up with a game plan for what I wanted to do with my life until I was pregnant and then had my baby.

That was when I knew what I didn't want to do with the rest of my life. In understanding that, I decided I needed to start mapping out what I actually wanted.

I couldn't see myself settling into the role of a stay-at-home mom. I know that women (and men) who choose to stay home and take care of their children have perhaps the most difficult job in the world. I would never disparage anyone making that choice that because it is a real full-time job, which I contemplated briefly while I was struggling through a few difficult months of pregnancy.

I admire women who do that. I love my son with all of my heart. But that wasn't an option for me. I know several women who are stay-at-home moms, and they love it. If that's what makes you happy, I say do it. But it wasn't something I could do. I needed a purpose that was all my own, goals to set and strive for, and the challenges of accomplishing what I set out to do in a career I loved.

Knowing what you *don't* like and knowing what you don't want to do with your life can be just as empowering as knowing what you're passionate about. So I sat down one evening and wrote out my plan on a piece of paper. It was simple.

"Get back to work."

"Get back on television."

"Appear or star in a couple of films over the next two years."

I hadn't done any movies at this point, but I knew I wanted to get into acting in film. So I wrote it down. I didn't have this elaborate PowerPoint presentation or some fancy vision board. I simple wrote down what I wanted for my career.

When I moved to Denver to be with Melo, who was playing for the Nuggets, I was happy with our relationship. But I was miserable feeling like I wasn't doing anything. I didn't like the idea of not having a purpose. I felt as if I was watching the whole world go by and I wasn't a part of it.

I needed to feel that I was moving in a forward direction. I needed to be back in the game. I needed to execute my plan.

Today, I have a yearly plan—what I hope to accomplish over the next twelve months. In 2014, my plan was to become a series regular. This season my role has increased from an occasional appearance to being in six out of ten episodes of *Power*. So while I'm not a recurring character, it's definitely one step closer to becoming a regular. I also wanted to appear in one or two movies during 2014. Check! I appeared in *Think Like a Man Too* and I wrapped *Destined*, which will be out in the summer of 2015. I also planned to have my clothing line picked up by a major retail store. (Still working on it.)

These are just a few of the goals I set for myself for 2014 that I focused my energies on accomplishing.

Having a plan or a vision is nothing unless you put power behind it. It's not enough to have goals; you also need to know how you're going to reach them. I wanted to star in movies. So I needed to hone my acting skills. I started taking classes.

I knew a few people who were actors and I asked them for advice on the best places to take acting classes. Living with an athlete, I know the importance of training. I didn't think I could just show up to an audition and that would be good enough. Even if I got the role, I wanted to be good. That would happen only with training.

Acting class is not only where I can learn the craft; it's also the best place to network, to find out where the new and hot opportunities are. Through acting classes I've also learned who are the real power players in the business— the directors, casting agents, producers, etc.—people who can help me reach my goals. I've also learned about the film festivals. It's the best place to meet people who are in my field from whom I can learn.

The people you need to make your goals and visions happen aren't just going to call you or walk up to you and hand you an opportunity. You have to go to them. And you must have a plan for how you will approach them. I talk about this in depth in the chapter on being persistent.

I usually map out and practice what I'm going to say because I don't want to babble or come off too nervous or rushed. I also make sure that my look is right. It all matters and it all requires planning. Don't just hastily rush into a situation thinking you have to seize the moment right now, because you won't get a second chance to make a good first impression.

My short-term plans usually revolve around my family. It's important that Kiyan and Melo are included in my day-to-day plans. When your family isn't written into your plans it can throw everything off balance. My schedule is about making sure there is time for them.

When making your plans and mapping out your vision, make sure you dream big. I love the saying: "Shoot for the moon. Even if you miss, you'll land among the stars." It's so true. If you dream big, even if you don't make it all the way there, where you end up will be so much farther ahead than if you didn't dream big at all.

My best example for someone in my life who dreamed big and exceeded his vision is Ludacris.

I feel most connected to his journey because I saw it unfold from the beginning. He also started as an intern at the Atlanta radio station just as I did, and he worked his way to being on the air, where he really shone. We co-hosted a show together called *Future Flavas* along with Poon Daddy.

I watched him dream of being a rapper, then make that dream into a concrete plan. He started making mixed tapes in hopes of getting a record deal. When no label would sign him to a deal, he didn't let that stop him. He would get in his car and sell his mixed tapes out of its trunk. The car, incidentally, is part of his story, too.

He talked about that Acura Legend in a promo he did. He's even rapped about it. He still owns and drives that car to this day because it symbolizes his journey.

I watched him say what he was going to do and far exceed all expectations. He then decided to take his music on the road.

I remember the day he came into the studio and announced he was leaving the station to pursue his dream. He had come in for our usual shift, which was six to ten, the most popular shift after the morning show. He was very excited.

"Yo, I'm going to get in my car and drive around the country and sell this joint out of the trunk of my car," he told us.

Luda was getting a lot of attention in the Atlanta area and within the music industry. Timbaland produced the single "Phat Rabbit," which became a hit. Then he wrote and performed a rap for a John Madden video game. But there was still no record deal with a major label. So he started his own label, Disturbing Tha Peace Records.

Ludacris never stop pursuing his dream. He was persistent. He also stuck to his plan. He wasn't waiting around for a major label to finally wake up and give him a deal he deserved. He started his own label and distributed his own music.

He even gave me an assist on his way out.

"You're talented," he told me. "You should try to find another job somewhere. Don't fall to the wayside because I'm not here."

I hadn't thought about what his leaving would mean for me. I didn't have a plan. Sometimes you need a nudge from someone to get busy. I realized that with Luda leaving in thirty days, they would replace him or replace the whole show. It would be hard to imagine our show without the three of us, together.

That very next day, I asked someone in production to put together an air check for me. It was four breaks with snippets of my best on-air performances, with some sound effects added to make it sound great. I then went into the room where they had the computers and resource books and found the book that listed every radio station and program director in the country. I labeled ten envelopes and stuck my air check and a cover letter in each envelope and mailed them out that day. Within two weeks I got the call from Los Angeles.

While the road to your plan may not be easy, if you have one and you stick to it, it can happen. The road leading to your ultimate goal may be filled with roadblocks and bumps. But don't quit. If the plan is solid, you will arrive there. I know Ludacris expected to be signed immediately. He had worked hard and his music was good. When that didn't happen, he didn't get discouraged. Instead, he found another route to get there. He went around the obstacle by creating a new path.

Sometimes when things don't fall in line with what I have planned—which happens from time to time—I have to take a moment and remember how it all started and what I'm working for. I take it back to the days of making a hundred and fifty dollars for club appearances and getting coffee and doing other menial tasks while interning and I remember that I did it all happily because I knew ultimately where I planned to be. Those rough patches and those days of struggling to make it were some of the best times of my life.

One of the best parts of having a plan is when you finally get to where you're going, look back and appreciate what you had to go through to get there. That's motivation for your next plan. But also, don't forget to smell the roses along the way and appreciate even the bumps and the obstacles.

You need to enjoy every part of your journey.

Find Your Own Power Path

Imagine for a minute that you are the best gardener in the world. You have a green thumb—everything you touch grows and blooms. You love to garden, and it makes you happy.

Then, someone comes along and tells you that football is so much better than gardening. If you really want to be someone, you have to be a football player. So you put on some pads, hit a training session or two, and get out on the field. Then a three-hundred-and-fifteen-pound linebacker comes barreling down the line and knocks you into next week. Suddenly, football isn't so great, and you realize that you should have stuck with gardening all along.

There are two ways to choose your career path: Follow others' expectations and examples or follow your own interests, talents, and passion. While the latter can be challenging, the first option almost always ends badly, like swapping gardening for football when your heart's not really in it. The most successful people in the world followed their own instincts and goals to achieve greatness, even when it was difficult or everyone told them they were crazy. You have certain gifts and skills for a reason. Put them to work for you and find your own power path. Asking some key questions can help you find it.

1. What would you do for free? I'm *not* saying that you should work for free. Your work has value and you should be compensated well for it. But what would you want to do just for the love of it? What makes you happy and excited? Your power path should be filled with the things you love to do every day, whether it's mixing music, building companies, or helping others. Find the things that bring you joy and make them part of the goal.

2. What do you do better than other people? Think about where you're most confident. Are there skills on which others have complimented you in the past? Are you known for being really good at something? Those could be clues to your power path. We tend to excel at the things we like to do. How can you take those skills and turn them into passion plays for your future?

3. When you daydream about your future, what does it look like? When you close your eyes and think about what you want your future to look like, what's there? Maybe a big family and a great job. You might dream of traveling around the world. Or maybe your dream is rooted in building a small business and being surrounded by a loving community of people. Your dream is unique to you and should never be compared with someone else's. Choose your own path.

4. How can you get there? At first, following your own path may seem impossible. It may seem like there are a million obstacles, including time, money, education, connections, you name it. But there's always a way to move closer to your goals.

Write down what you want to accomplish, along with all the steps it's going to take to get there. Don't worry if the list is long. Just start tackling the steps one by one. You'll be surprised at the opportunities that arise once you start taking positive action toward what you were meant to do. It may not be easy, but it will be worth it.

CHAPTER THREE

The Power of Fear

Fearlessness requires attention and receptivity—
it takes focus to stand in the still eye of a tornado
and not be swept away by it.

—Susan Piver (bestselling author of
The Hard Questions)

What separates people who are successful from people who spend their lives wishing and hoping something magical will happen but somehow never does, is fear.

I don't know a single person who isn't afraid of something at some point in their lives. Some of us have very real fears—physical danger or fear of consequences from something we may have done. But most of us have fears that are simply in our heads. Fear that we will not be liked or loved, fear that we aren't good enough, fear that we will fail. That last one is the biggest made-up fear that most of us have. Fear of failure.

That fear prevents us from taking chances, stops us from believing we can make the leap to a new career or higher position, and keeps us from acting with confidence in everything we do, both personally and professionally. If we can conquer just that fear, many of us will see so many great things happen in our lives.

One definition of courage is being afraid and doing it anyway. Courage is the act. Power is the result of that act. When you face your fears and plow through them in spite of being afraid, what happens on the other side is that you gain power. You build your power muscle every time you do something you were afraid to do. And before you know it, your fear will be replaced with a source of power that you will be able to tap into anytime you need it.

I went on safari in the summer of 2014. It was my first time in Africa and we visited one of the most beautiful reserves in the world. Animals from throughout the animal kingdom just roamed freely.

On one of our drives through the reserve, an elephant put his head into our Jeep. It was an open Jeep, but he was so close. And I was petrified. Have you ever seen an elephant up close? You think you know how big an elephant is, but you have no idea until you're literally face-to-face with one. This elephant could have overturned our Jeep in one motion. He could have crushed it. I just put my scarf over my head and prayed. We were at his mercy. We all kept very still. No one moved. No one said a word.

He eventually satisfied his curiosity and moved on.

I was powerless in that moment. But when the moment passed, I learned something about fear. In that moment I had absolutely no control over the outcome. I couldn't prevent that elephant from turning over our vehicle. I was helpless against his power. So I let go. I let go of my fears and insecurities and embraced the moment.

Kiyan was in the Jeep with us. And he was way calmer than I was. He was quietly taking it all in. I don't think he could understand all of the possibilities of what could have gone wrong. But that's the point. While I had my scarf over my head praying, Kiyan was able to really take in and experience it all because he wasn't thinking about the worst-case scenarios over which he had no control to begin with.

How often in life do we worry ourselves senseless about things over which we have no control? How often do we allow fear to keep us from experiencing something in life? How often do we allow our perception of our own powerlessness, insecurities, and weaknesses get in the way of learning something or growing?

I gleaned all of that in that moment . . . *after* the elephant left.

And I was able to reflect on the moments in my own life when I allowed fear to stunt my growth.

I was nineteen years old when I dropped out of Howard University because of a guy. I wrote extensively about this man in *The Love Playbook* and how I allowed a relationship, a man, to chart my course and run my young life. When we had finally broken up, I was devastated. So much so, I couldn't stand to be in the same town with him. I left school and moved home to Atlanta with my mother. And I was scared.

The fear wasn't about the future of my career because I dropped out of college. I realized early that in my major, Communications, I already had enough real-world experience to work in my field of choice—radio. I had learned more than I could in any class by actually working in my internship and being an on-air personality at WHTA. For someone who had zero radio experience, those communications classes would have been very valuable. But they weren't as much for me. I wasn't afraid that I wouldn't get a job because I dropped out. My fear centered on being alone. I was afraid that I wouldn't have the life I envisioned because I didn't have that man. I was afraid that I'd never find someone to love me again.

For two weeks after I returned home, I moped around the house, depressed, crying all of the time. I even contemplated calling him to convince him to get back together with me, as crazy as that sounds. Right after a breakup, you're very vulnerable and apt to make bad decisions.

You're sad and lonely and you start to rethink everything. You start second-guessing your decision, asking if you did the right thing.

Toward the end of that second week of wallowing in my own sorrow I had a conversation with myself.

"Are you going to let this breakup ruin and determine your entire future?" I asked myself.

I had checked in with a few friends back in DC and discovered that he was getting on just fine. He may have been sad about the breakup but he was still working on the air at his radio station, still doing his club dates, and still living his life. He wasn't letting this breakup stop what he was doing. While he was moving on, I was in bed not wanting to talk to anyone or do anything.

Knowing that he was able to move on with his life empowered me to do the same. It became my motivation.

Whenever any of us was going through something in my family, my grandmother always used to say, "Wake up and throw some cold water on your face and everything will be okay."

So that's what I did. I got up the next day, threw some cold water on my face, and decided to get it together. I put my sadness and my fear of being alone on the back burner and focused on the life that was in front of me.

Today is a new day. Enough!

When one area isn't working for you, you must find

another power source. Find that place to recharge yourself. For some people, it's spending time with their family. For others, it may be spending time alone meditating.

I've always been able to tap into my power in one place, in particular—work. Whenever things weren't going well in my personal life, I could always count on working to pull me through. It's always been my go-to power place.

That Monday when I got up and splashed cold water on my face, the next thing I did was call my old boss at WHTA and see if there was a spot for me. It was time to restart my career in radio and get back to doing what I loved. Don't get me wrong—I was afraid to make the call. What if they didn't have a position for me? What if they simply didn't want me back? But as I let those negative thoughts seep in, I quickly realized I had to be willing to do whatever it took to go back.

WHTA's general manager Mary Catherine Sneed took my call. I told her I'd be willing to work wherever I was needed. I didn't expect to jump right back into my old job, and I was willing to work myself back up to that position again. I was honest with her and I told her that I felt that I went to school for all of the wrong reasons, and I needed to be back on the air. But if that position wasn't available, I'd do whatever was available.

Mary Catherine was really understanding. She totally got that college wasn't for everyone and she didn't judge me. She didn't look at me like a dropout loser. And she didn't make me sweat.

"Welcome back!" she said.

She told me there had been a void since I left. There were no women on the air doing what I had been doing, and they hadn't found anyone who could fill my shoes. In addition to being a woman, I also hit both the Latino and African-American markets. But the reason I was rehired on the spot was because of my work ethic, she said. Nobody put in the kind of work I had when I was there and she remembered that.

I'd made a few power plays that made my coming back a whole lot easier.

1. I left a good impression. I was not just remembered, I was missed. I worked so hard while I was there that it was easy for Mary Catherine to invite me back.

2. I left graciously. I was leaving for school, not because I was unhappy or because I found another job. But even if I had been leaving for another professional opportunity, I would have gone out in the same way. As I left, I was very thankful to Chaka Zulu, Mary Catherine, and all of the people who helped me while I was there. I let them all know how much I appreciated them. And that served me well when it was time to come back. (For more on exiting with grace, see Chapter Four.)

3. I was humble. I didn't expect to just be hired back. I didn't approach it with a sense of entitlement. I believe having a humble attitude goes a long way; it can be one of your greatest sources of power. For some, power is a matter of strength and overt will. But real power is often found in the little things—in your attitude and how you carry yourself. I was humble and hungry at the same time.

I started back at WHTA the following Monday and it took me about a month to get back in the flow. My life became about work. The more I worked, the less I thought about him. I was all about my shift and then hosting club dates and getting back to focusing on my goals and dreams. Work was my therapy. It brought back my sanity. Through work I regained my power and before I knew it, I even regained my joy.

That year after dropping out of Howard University was pivotal for me. So many wonderful things began to happen for me. It also propelled me to make even bolder decisions. After a couple of months of living at home, I decided to move out and find my own place.

Again, I was scared. I had never really lived on my own. I had gone from Mother's house to Howard, where room and board was covered (and where I eventually moved in with "him," who took care of all of the expenses). I never really had the responsibilities of taking care of myself and paying my own bills. I had no clue how I was going to afford it. I was working again, but not making a whole lot of money. There was real fear about being able to afford it. But I knew if I had to take on more club appearances and work even harder, I was willing to do it.

I didn't leave because I needed to get out of my mom's house. It was actually cool living with her. Moving out was simply about wanting to be an adult and feeling empowered. You aren't officially an adult until you are living on your own, paying your own bills, and being responsible. Until you do that, you're playing at adulthood. I believe everyone needs to have that experience. Some people move straight from their mother's house into a relationship with someone. That's not the same. Even if it's for a brief period, everyone needs to know what it feels like to have to make rent, or else.

I was scared about that. But that fear and pressure made me work harder and made me more focused. It gave me a reason to succeed. I knew I couldn't tell my landlord, "I don't have the rent this month." And I knew my mom and dad really didn't have it to pay it for me. I had no safety net. So I had to create one for myself through my work.

After I got my old job back, and I knew I would have a steady paycheck, my friend 4 Ize (who also rapped with Ludacris) and I decided we would get a place together. We drove around the city and saw signs for apartments for lease. We settled on a place that was close to the radio station and also to the studio where he was making his music.

It was in a decent neighborhood, but the must-have was a cheap price (something I could afford without him, to be honest).

While I knew I could totally handle the rent, what I didn't factor in were some of the other expenses associated with living on your own—like utilities, cable, and furniture. Four Eyes and I didn't have a living room couch, no end tables, nothing. We had a bunch of pillows on the floor and a big television that he brought with him. We had a television but no television stand.

I slept on the floor of my bedroom for a week with blankets and pillows until I got my first paycheck and was able to buy a bed. I had always wanted a waterbed, so that's what I got. It turns out that the idea of a waterbed is so much cooler than actually having to sleep on one.

The bed was the biggest purchase I made. I wasn't interested in buying things. I was more interested in building—my savings and my career.

For my next big career move I again had to work through my fear. Leaving for Los Angeles was one of the scariest days of my life. As I was packing, I was talking to myself.

Wow, it's Hollywood. It's a big deal. You're going to be a part of something great.

Then I started asking myself the tough questions.

Will you be able to perform at this next level? Will you be good enough?

I was comfortable in Atlanta. It was home. I had a support system there with my family and friends and everyone at the station. They all looked out for me. I was the little sister people wanted to take care of. Coming there so young, it seemed as if they felt responsible for me. Now I was going to this big market—one of the top in the country—three thousand miles away from home to a place where I knew no one. This was the big time. A major corporate station. This was not a game.

Yes, I was afraid. There was fear of failure, fear of being away from home, and fear of being alone.

Again, power is the result of courage. You can tap into it only when you decide to be afraid yet do it anyway. It was a job, work, something in which I always found comfort. I would just put my head down and work my ass off and watch the rest fall into place. I used that fear as fuel and I put it in my work tank and took it all to Los Angeles, where I saw myself rising to the top as I had always done.

Los Angeles was an opportunity. I had an opportunity to prove myself and prove *to* myself that what I felt inside—that I was made to be on the radio—was actually true. My mom was also there to keep me pushing forward.

Every power player needs an accomplice, a mentor, a supporter, someone in his or her corner. For me, among others, that person has always been my mom. My mother is the personification of support. She was even there with me on the plane ride to Los Angeles and stayed with me for a couple of days while I settled into corporate housing and into my new job and city. She could stay only a couple of days because she had to work. I was still just a teenager and while I was very independent, having my mom there even for that short time made the transition a little easier. I wish she could have been there longer, though.

When my mother left, I was like Alice in Wonderland without the wonderland. I was completely alone and the fear set in again. Again I did what I did best when unsure and afraid—I poured myself into my work. I was at the radio station all of the time, taking on every club hosting job that came our way. Slowly, I got to know a few people, like S. Dot, who worked in the sales department. She took me under her wing and helped me learn this new city.

I was alone and insecure. But in that moment, I was my most powerful. You have the greatest potential for success when you're able to overcome your fears and push through.

I had to make it work. I had to perform. There was no way I was running back to Atlanta with my tail between my legs. Failure wasn't an option. I had to make friends and be successful. I had to push through my fear. Actually, my fear of failure far outweighed my fear of being alone. That, too, gave me power.

A couple of months after I started, the station was purchased. When this happens in radio, usually everything changes. The new management either changes the format, for example, from hip-hop to pop. Or the new management brings in their own people to host the shows. It almost always means that jobs and positions will be lost.

The day after the station was purchased, I was called into the office by the new management team. I was nervous as hell, thinking, "This is it." Then I talked to myself. I reminded myself that just as I was bold enough to send out air checks around the country to get this job in Los Angeles, I could do it again to go somewhere else if I had to.

I had in my mind that I was talented and I was young. I *would* find another position. Somewhere. Fortunately, I didn't have to. Instead of firing me, I received what was in my mind a promotion. I was moved from midday to the evening drive slot. Some people wouldn't say that was a promotion. But for me it was a better fit for where I wanted to be and for the audience I was relating to.

I went from a shift that started at ten in the morning when my audience was primarily stay-at-home moms and an older demographic that happened to be home during that time, to *my* demographic—young people, the after-school crowd, the club set.

I was on from six until ten in the evening and it was huge. It was a time slot when I could shine. The audience was different, the music was different, the vibe was different. We even had a deejay spinning for an hour of our show. I got a partner for this shift named Eric Cubiche. I came up with a cute name for us—The B Syde.

Back in the day when you'd get a mixed tape in the industry, there was the regular side, or A Side, which was where the commercial music was. Then there was the B Side, which was the risqué or edgier music. Most people on the streets thought the B Side was always better, had the most innovative music. It was the hidden treasure. That's how I saw Eric and me. And it resonated with our audience. We became very popular very quickly.

I was living my dream. Making my own way in Los Angeles and succeeding in a big market. I was proud of what I'd accomplished and knew that it was only through overcoming what scared me the most that I was able to follow my dreams.

After being on the radio in Los Angeles less than two years, TV—more specifically MTV—came calling.

When I think back, most of my successes have come on the heels of being afraid to do something and then talking myself into doing it anyway.

Like getting my internship at the radio station in Atlanta, for starters. I was underage with no experience and yet I rationalized to myself that I had nothing to lose. I lied about my age and experience and presented to the people in charge of hiring that I would be great for the job. It was scary and they could have seen right through me. If that had happened, I might not have ever had that opportunity again. It worked and the rest is history. But I was scared at first.

The relationship between fear and power in most of our lives is very close. Most of us quit or don't try because of our fears. And some, like me, plow ahead despite the fear. My fear was never big enough for me not to know the benefit. I knew in order to get ahead, I had to make this move. That's how I approach everything.

Everything! From riding roller coasters to zip lining to skydiving to taking a role that may seem over my head. I've done it all. Been scared to death to do it. But I never wanted fear to stop me.

Overcoming fear is power.

I have a friend who was offered a tremendous opportunity in a new company, paying double what she was making. But the job would take her away from her man. She was afraid that if she took the job she would lose her man. So her fear cost her what could have been the career move of a lifetime. I know quite a few women who let a relationship, or fear of losing it, get in the way of their career opportunities. It's paralyzing.

Sometimes I think it's not even the relationship they're afraid of losing. They use it as an excuse to cover the real fear—fear of failing.

I have also seen too many who haven't pursued their dreams and are sitting around with regrets to this day. I never wanted to be that person.

I also have seen some great examples of fearlessness and power. One of my best examples was my grandmother, who has always been a big inspiration in my life—someone who always seemed to have the right answers. She had what I describe as quiet power. You know it when you're around someone like that because they just command respect. But her story, her life is an example of facing and overcoming adversity and making it work. I keep her with me and tap into my grandmother's power whenever I need that extra push. She's always there for me.

My mom told me she asked her mother, when she was on her deathbed, "Mom, would you have done anything different?"

She said, "I would not change anything in my life."

That was so meaningful to me. That said that she had no regrets and that she stood by whatever decisions she made. Everything you do in life is a lesson—even the mistakes. They set the table and prepare you for whatever is to come next.

My mom has also been a great example of power in my life because she's so different from me. I use her to bounce things off of, but also as a compass to make sure I'm doing the right thing. My mom is more cautious than I am. She's not so quick to take a chance. She says she wishes she didn't always play it so safe and that she didn't talk herself out of so many things. Not that she had a bad life, but she missed out on some experiences. I think that's why she never held me back from doing something—not once. She pushed me to do the things that she didn't do. And I appreciate that. So in many ways my mother fostered the power in me that she may not have been able to use in her own life.

I never wanted to look back over my life and wish I had done something but didn't because I was afraid.

Power Plays to Master Any Presentation

One of the biggest fears most people have is public speaking. I know people who are literally paralyzed by the prospect of having to stand in front of a crowd and give a speech or presentation. Ironically, a lot of actors are shy and are uncomfortable speaking publicly. They're cool in front of a camera, but having to speak before a couple of hundred or thousands will make some physically ill.

But presentations and speeches can be very important depending on where you want to go in your career. Don't let your fear of speaking or presenting hold you back. This is an easy fear to overcome. You just need to know the right plays.

Tips for Overcoming a Fear
of Public Speaking

1. Know your stuff. Nothing will make you more confident in speaking in front of others than knowing your material cold. When you are well versed and passionate about your topic, virtually nothing can throw you. So, be sure you've really studied the material you'll be covering. If you need help, have a coworker or team member help you prep, including coming up with questions that the audience might ask so that you're prepared for them.

2. Rehearse. Practice your presentation or speech until you're sure you've mastered it. Try pausing in different places and emphasizing key points. It might help to practice in front of a mirror or video record yourself so that you can work out the kinks. Try not to rely on pages of paper or dense PowerPoint decks because you'll be too tempted to read off of them instead of speaking from the heart, which makes you more effective.

3. Look fierce. We know that people judge us by how we look. Wear something that makes you feel confident. That doesn't necessarily mean going out and spending big bucks on a new designer outfit. Choose the pieces in your closet that make you feel good about yourself. When you're not worried about what you're wearing, you've eliminated a big distraction that can undermine your confidence.

4. Find a friendly face. Get to the engagement early and talk to a few people there. Once you've made a friendly connection, seek out those faces in the room if you get nervous. Seeing a friendly face in the crowd can calm your nerves. Also, remember that people are generally rooting for you to succeed. They're in the room because they want to hear what you have to say.

5. Speak up. Be sure to breathe deeply during your talk and project your voice. You don't want to shout, but you want to be sure that everyone can hear you. Whispery voices sound like they lack confidence, which can hurt your message.

6. Be yourself. If you're a funny person, make an appropriate joke. If you are a just-the-facts person, use your ability to be succinct. But don't try to be someone you're not, especially while you're making an important presentation. You'll appear more confident if you let your natural personality shine through. After all, you're pretty amazing. It's time to show that to others.

CHAPTER FOUR

The Power of Gratitude

Gratitude unlocks the fullness of life. It turns what we have into enough, and more. It turns denial into acceptance, chaos to order, confusion to clarity. It can turn a meal into a feast, a house into a home, a stranger into a friend.

—Melody Beattie

In 2012, I appeared in a movie, *Think Like a Man*, loosely based on the Steve Harvey bestselling book, *Act Like a Lady, Think Like a Man*. I had to audition for the role, which is the norm. The auditions were in Los Angeles and I wouldn't have time to fly out, so I taped my audition of the "sides" or the scenes they wanted me to act out, and sent it the producers. I was hoping for one of the main roles.

They told me I didn't get the role I was auditioning for, but they wanted me to come out to Los Angeles to audition for one of the smaller parts.

Now I could have had an attitude about being passed over for the role I wanted. And I could have been sour enough to not want to go all the way out to Los Angeles in hopes of getting a smaller part. But I was grateful for the opportunity. I had never really been in a major film before this and I was willing to play a water girl, if it meant being in the film.

When I arrived in Los Angeles, I had to audition for the producer Will Packer (*Stomp the Yard*, *Takers*, *This Christmas*, just to name a few), the director Tim Story (most known for directing *Barbershop* and *The Fantastic Four*), and a room full of power players. These were the people who could and would make the final decision about who would be in the film. My legs were literally shaking when I walked in that room. But I kept talking to myself to calm down. I knew all I had to do was perform to the best of my abilities. And I did.

I got the call a couple of days later that I got the role of Sonia, the best friend of Mya, who was Meagan Good's character.

While filming, I met and became friendly with the amazing cast—Taraji P. Henson and Michael Ealy, Regina Hall and Terrence J, Meagan Good and Romany Malco, Gabrielle Union and Jerry Ferrara, Gary Owen and Kevin

Hart. I also became really close with Will Packer and Tim Story. We had a blast on the set and everyone worked really well together.

My role was small. I was in just a couple of scenes. During publicity for the film, we heard there would be a part two, *Think Like a Man Too*. Everyone was excited, but I didn't know if I would be asked back. The film was about two of the characters getting married and everyone was coupled up. In the first movie, my character didn't have a mate. So it would be very easy for them to simply write me out of the next part.

But they did ask me back. When I thanked Will for inviting me to appear in the next movie, he said, "You were so easy to work with. You were so humble, so kind, why wouldn't we bring you back!"

Not only was I in the sequel, my role was expanded and I appeared throughout the entire movie, instead of being in a scene here or there the way I was in the first film. I was even on the promotional poster!

I know I did a good job with my small role, but what got me in the sequel wasn't just my performance. There are plenty of people who can put in a good performance. The deciding factor, and this was what I was told, was that I was so easy and fun to work with.

That started with gratitude. I was so grateful for the opportunity that I couldn't help but show it to everyone. And in return, I was rewarded with more opportunities.

They say nice guys finish last. But my experience has taught me just the opposite.

In business, especially, I'm learning more and more that being nice, humble, and gracious will take you far. I've learned that there is a lot of power in being gracious.

I met with my manager and her team recently, who are working on branding. She said, "La, you're one of the few people who always remember to say thank you. You're one of the few people who are appreciative. That makes us want to work harder for you."

I've always understood that. But it wasn't something anyone had to teach me. It comes as second nature.

I was raised in a family of nice people. My grandmother, who raised her children in the Marcy Projects in Brooklyn, was known for leaving her door unlocked. People in the building knew this. It wouldn't be unusual for my mom or uncles to come home from school to find a neighbor in the house eating.

My grandmother felt that if people needed something, they should be able to just come. My mom would come home and would see a stranger and say, "Who is that?" And my grandmother would say, "Don't judge. They needed something to eat." That was just how she was.

Being gracious should be something that comes naturally. It shouldn't be forced. People will know if you're not genuinely gracious. If it feels inauthentic, that can backfire and make people not trust you and your motives. But I believe practice makes perfect. Work on it in situations with everyday people until it becomes second nature. You can train yourself to be more gracious and nice just by practicing it.

Try these simple ways to express gratitude:

- Write a note.

Take a moment to consider your life over the last year, and write down all of the people for whom you're truly grateful. Think about your interactions. Send a card only to those who you can genuinely say you're grateful for. Be authentic and real. Be true. It doesn't have to be the holidays to send a card as long as the message is genuine. A handwritten note would be even better.

- Create a kind culture.

Think about those around you and create an environment of kindness and mutual respect. Small acts of basic kindness can go a long way to make someone else's day a little bit better. Try, for example, holding the elevator for someone running to catch it. It might take you an extra few seconds to reach your destination, but it helped them out. Or, if you're making a midmorning coffee run, offer to get a cup for someone else on your team or in your office.

• Give thoughtful gifts.

An unexpected and thoughtful gift to express your appreciation can go a long way. It's not about the cost here, either. It can be flowers, a gift card, something that lets a person know you thought about them.

In the workplace, be selective about how you show gratitude. Sending gifts and cards to your bosses can be tricky. I wouldn't do it. It can come off wrong. And having a misstep at the top can totally backfire. It's best to do nothing. Let your work and your workplace demeanor carry you far as it relates to your bosses. Unless, of course, you have a close relationship. These moments will have to be played by ear.

• Say hello.

Expressing gratitude can be as simple as saying good morning to people at your job—from the security guard to the people who clean the building. It costs nothing to be pleasant.

It's not something I have to think about. I've always felt that if people are working on your behalf, you should be nice. If you are seeking help from someone or a job or an opportunity you catch more flies with honey. Even with fans, I always want to be gracious. Sometimes being kind to strangers is more important than being kind to those you know.

I never understood people who make it big and then are mean and standoffish. The old saying is that money magnifies. I have watched people find success and become the biggest jerks. You see them on the sets of movies and their room or trailer has to be way on the other side of everyone else's because they don't want to be bothered. And it's usually people who aren't even as big as they think they are.

That's the joke. The A-listers, some of the biggest superstars, are the nicest people. Tom Cruise has that reputation. I've heard that he will just walk up to fans and introduce himself (as if there's a person alive who doesn't know who Tom Cruise is) and shake their hand. He's legendary in the business for being just a nice guy.

Someone else who has that same reputation for being easy to work with is Will Smith. Will has said, "I've trained myself to illuminate the things in my personality that are likable and to hide and protect the things that are less likable."

That says a few things to me. It takes work or training to be nice or highlight the "likable" things about you. Some people have just a pleasant personality. But what Will is saying is that if you don't or even if you do, you should practice and train yourself to be even more likable. The other thing that statement says to me is that there must be a great payoff for being likable. Or why do it? For Will Smith and perhaps Tom Cruise, they have identified the power in being pleasant, kind, and likable as a key to their success.

Working at MTV all of those years I got to see people on the way up and on the way out. I've seen new artists come to our show on TRL with a dozen hangers-on and handlers and really acting full of themselves. Then I've seen someone like Jamie Foxx show up by himself and he's hanging with the cameramen and the interns before his appearance on air, cutting up and making everyone laugh. Gracious.

How you navigate things you don't like in your workplace is also important. The conditions can be horrible and while no one should deal with injustices and a bad work environment, *how* you deal with it will determine your success there.

When I'm on set, I may run into a line in the script or a scene that I don't understand. Now I can go in and tell the director, "I don't get this! This sucks!" Or I can ask if he has a few moments and tell him I'd like for him to help me see the scene better. I enlist him in helping me work through it, instead of putting him on the defensive.

"I'm not really comfortable with this scene," I may say. "How can we make this work better?"

I thank him for his time and I tell him how I appreciate him sharing his knowledge. If I do it that way, he will be more inclined to change the scene that I'm uncomfortable with and not see me as being difficult. Diplomacy. Graciousness.

When dealing with people, it's always better to focus on the good they bring to the table, when attempting to tackle something that needs fixing. Put the compliments first. Put the things they're good at first.

If that person is your boss, you have to figure out how to approach him or her without ruffling feathers. Plan out what you're going to say and ask yourself, "How will this be perceived?" or "Is there a better way to say this?" Come up with the better way.

When I hear, "La, you're one of the few people who everyone says, 'She's so cool and easy to work with,'" that's the highest compliment.

It has always been important to me that people have a good impression of me. While I don't care what people think on Twitter, Instagram, or social media, I care deeply what producers, directors, casting agents, and my fellow actors think of me. These are the professionals that know me and know my work, and I value their opinions.

I have seen what having a bad reputation has done to careers. There was one actress who was getting a lot of work in movies after appearing on a hit television series. She was one of the hottest actresses during this time. But her reputation of being difficult, nasty, and just not a good person started getting around Hollywood. Soon, she was off her television show and you stopped seeing her in movies.

I saw her in a small commercial several years later and thought, "Wow, how far has she fallen."

But I also thought, "This can be fixed." It's never too late to change your reputation as long as you're willing to be humble.

If you're known for being nasty, change it—even if you believe you are simply misunderstood and people have judged you wrongly. I have met people who have had a bad reputation and I found them to be the coolest people. They may not even know what's being said about them behind their back. But if you aren't getting ahead the way you believe you should or you aren't getting great feedback from those in positions to hire you—you might need to work on your nice game.

If you're perceived negatively, you have to work to change the perception. Reach out to people. Be accessible. Here are some simple steps. Smile. Say hello to people. Everyone. Start reaching out to people you don't normally reach out to just to check in and see how they're doing.

Invite peers or people you work with to lunch or coffee. It's the little things that go a long way.

You can change the perception people have of you by just working on yourself and practicing being nice. People will love to start seeing you differently and talking about the change. Everyone loves a comeback story.

Being nice always wins.

Being gracious is not just about smiling and being nice, though. It's also about your attitude when faced with adversity. If you're having a tough day at home, do you bring it to work and involve everyone in your drama? If you're having a tough day at the office, does everyone know about it? While people may appear to be sympathetic, you more often than not come off as pathetic, not powerful, when you wear your emotions—particularly the negative ones—on your sleeve.

Your Exit Is as Important as Your Entrance

How you leave a situation—an interview or even a job—is important. When leaving a job—even if you're fired—it's important that you leave with grace. Give your old boss a thank-you note letting him or her know what you learned while there and thanking them for the opportunity—even if you can't stand them. I'm sure you can find one or two things you learned. It shouldn't be insincere. Just dig deep to find the positives and put it in a note. I would do a handwritten card. But you can send an e-mail. If there were coworkers who helped you along the way, I would send them a nice little note, too. No matter what went down during your time there, your last impression will usually be a lasting impression. Always leave people with a good feeling about you. Whether you quit or are fired, you will leave an impression that will follow you—good, bad, or indifferent. I always prefer the good. It's just common courtesy to thank people for their time after an interview and for their support over the years if you're leaving a job.

There was a story in late 2014 about an Alaskan television newscaster who literally quit on the air. "Fuck it, I quit!" she said and walked off during a live broadcast, leaving her fellow newscasters dumbfounded and scrambling for words. This story got a lot of traction and many people thought it was funny. Some even gave her the thumbs-up because she had the balls to do that.

But all I thought was, "She'll never work in television again." I wondered if it was really worth it to go out like that.

When you do something like that—cuss out a boss, or do some very public display when you quit—you will have a million hype men around you telling you how cool that was or how you made this big statement. But they won't be there when you're struggling to find that next job. And they won't be there to tell you how that will hurt you in the long run.

While that may have seemed empowering in the moment—and it was definitely bold—it was a bad move that will likely follow her for the rest of her life. She may go on to become a successful businesswoman, which she was leaving the network to do. But she will always be remembered for that moment and if she ever wanted to be a serious journalist in the future, she pretty much shut the door to that.

Power is the ability to maximize your opportunities, not diminish them. Something may seem cool in the moment or even in the times in which we live, but you need to be able to see long term and how your actions will play out. And while you're going out in a blaze of glory, you're also setting fire to bridges and no doubt countless opportunities that you may never know were there.

Remember, your exit is as important as your entrance. This goes for jobs, personal relationships, and even professional relationships.

I used a particular accounting firm for a number of years. They were great. But as my business grew and diversified, I found that I needed something different to take me to that next level. Now, I could have simply sent them a letter telling them I was moving on. Or I could have said nothing and just had one of my reps or my new accounting firm reach out to have my documents transferred.

I would have personally preferred that because I hate disappointing people and I am especially horrible at firing people. When I was younger I used to stay in bad business relationships with lawyers, managers, etc.—longer than I needed to—simply because I didn't want to let anyone down. But that's also not good business and it shows a lack of power.

So I knew, despite being nervous and anxious, I had to make that call to my old accounting firm.

When I called, the person I had been dealing with for several years answered and when I told him I was leaving his firm, he said he was sorry to hear I was leaving, but he was very cool about it. (He, too, must have understood the importance of a good exit.) He was so nice and under-standing that it made moving on so easy. He didn't even ask why I was leaving. He said he would contact the new firm and would be available to answer any of their ques-tions. He made the transition for me so easy.

I sent him flowers and wine and a thank-you note for being so good to me over the years in handling my money. I heard through the grapevine through mutual friends what he said about me after that: "La left us, but she was classy on the way out."

Saying "please" and "thank you" may seem like lost sentiments these days. But they are part of the vocabulary of every powerful person I know. Take nothing for granted and let people know you appreciate the things they do for you, no matter how small.

People in service jobs especially need to understand

this. It seems as if it would be common sense that if you're working in a field where you are taking care of the public—like a waiter, a gas station attendant, a grocery store checkout clerk, a toll collector, or a barista at a coffee shop, for example—that you should be nice and pleasant. But I have seen too many cases, especially of late, where people whose business it is to serve have the worst attitudes.

You never know who you are serving in those positions. A kind word can change your life. But beyond that, it's your job. If you don't like your job, you cannot take it out on the customers. And if you don't like your job, having a bad attitude won't help you get a better job. Just the opposite. It could lead to you losing the job you have or never seeing a promotion.

My dad has been a flight attendant forever. His job is very service-oriented and he runs into some of the nastiest people alive. He's told me horror stories about some of the people who have been drunk, nasty, or just downright rude to him. How does he handle it?

"I kill them with kindness," he told me.

My dad has the perfect demeanor to deal with all kinds of people. He's calm and controlled and compassionate.

"Me getting upset will just ruin my day," he said. "Those unpleasant moments with people are temporary. There are so many wonderful moments to focus on."

Kill Them with Kindness

That's a major power move. It disarms people—especially people who are being nasty. How do you continue with that behavior when met with a smile and a pleasant attitude on the other end? There's way more power in being nice than fighting nastiness with anger.

It's easy to be nice to people who are nice to you. It takes practice and work to be nice when people are nasty. Try it next time someone pisses you off or is rude or nasty. Instead of telling them off, smile and be nice. See what happens. And by doing it, you also lower your stress levels. You disarm them and you maintain your composure. Win-win.

People have the wrong perception of power, especially in business. A lot of people feel that you have to be mean, or ruthless, or be a bitch to get to the top. So they mimic what they see in these movies like *Wall Street*. Yes, there are plenty of successful people who happen to be jerks. But they aren't successful *because* they're jerks, but rather in spite of being jerks.

The biggest, most powerful people I know personally are the nicest. The rest—those with the big entourages, the unreasonable demands for appearances, those with bad attitudes—are pretenders. Your talent may take you to a place. But if your attitude is messed up, people will be waiting for you to fall and some will even throw banana peels in your path to make that fall happen quicker.

You'd rather have people fighting to help you succeed, instead of wishing for your failure.

I have gotten so many jobs just because the director or casting agent liked me. I know because they've told me. Being liked can sometimes take you a whole lot farther in life than just being talented.

But there is a difference between being liked and having power. Being a people pleaser and a doormat is being powerless. Don't let your kindness be a weakness. Use your kindness and gratitude as a tool to get ahead. Understand the power in being nice and gracious, without giving away your power by allowing people to use you. I'm not talking about going out of your way to serve people or be that one who always says yes. I'm talking simply about being gracious, making sure you honor those around you.

And by honoring others, you are actually honoring yourself.

Thinking Thankfully

- Be thankful, not indebted.

There's a huge difference between being grateful and thankful and feeling that you owe someone something. If you feel that you have to pay someone back immediately for doing something for you, then you aren't grateful. Gratitude to me means you are grateful but you don't owe anything in return. Accept the act of kindness. And if you do something for someone you shouldn't expect anything in return. If you do, then it's not really done in the right spirit. Make sure you check yourself. If the act is something you feel must be repaid immediately, then it is not being received well. Being grateful means also learning how to receive. That even goes for compliments. Learn to accept compliments. Receive them. Say thank you and move on.

• Gratitude in moderation.

Don't become a gratitude-a-holic. Every kind act doesn't have to be met with a response by you. And you don't have to go around thanking and being gracious to everybody. Pick and choose your moments when you get the greatest value. Remember, you don't want to be a doormat or a pushover. They say too much of a good thing can be bad. That goes for being gracious, too. Everything in moderation.

• Turn negativity into gratitude.

At some point in your life you will face tragedy— the loss of a job, the loss of an opportunity, even the loss of a loved one. That's all part of life. But how you handle these difficult times is so important. When you're going through it, just remember how it has been and how bad it could be and be grateful. There are people who are homeless, hungry, and suffering throughout the world. Remind yourself of your blessings and you will always stay in a place of gratitude.

CHAPTER FIVE

The Power of Persistence

Nothing in this world can take the place of persistence. Talent will not; nothing is more common than unsuccessful men with talent. Genius will not; unrewarded genius is almost a proverb. Education will not; the world is full of educated derelicts. Persistence and determination alone are omnipotent.

—Calvin Coolidge

I heard about a new television series debuting in summer of 2014 on the Starz network called, of all things, *Power*. The show is about a drug dealer who worked his way to the top to become a successful and respected legitimate businessman. It's a great plot with a strong cast, and I really wanted a shot at a role on the show.

The show's executive producer was Curtis Jackson

(aka 50 Cent). In 2010, we worked on an independent film together, *Gun* starring Val Kilmer. Curtis wrote, produced, and starred in it, and it was filmed in Grand Rapids, Michigan. We became pretty cool during the filming and stayed in touch a bit afterward. But we knew each other from way before then. I first met him when he was promoting *Get Rich or Die Tryin'*, 50's debut album. He came up to MTV and we became friends then. We talk frequently and are really good friends.

Curtis has always been a stand-up guy and a man of his word, so I decided to reach out to him about *Power*. If there was a role for me, he would tell me. If I wasn't right for any of them, I knew he would tell me that, too.

I didn't have his new number (he changes it every other week and while we talk frequently, we hadn't talked since he changed his number). But I tracked him down through a mutual friend. When I called, it went straight to voice mail. Instead of leaving a message, I texted him: "I really want a chance to audition for *Power*."

I told him what I wanted. I wasn't vague. I didn't just say, "Call me."

I know people think if they tell you what they want, you may not call them back. Well, if you don't tell them what you want, they probably won't call back *and* they'll be annoyed with you.

By communicating exactly what I wanted, I enabled 50 to be prepared when we did talk. He offered me the chance for an audition, but he was quick to tell me that there were no guarantees that I would get the job. There was a casting team in place and I had to kill my audition to get the job. He could get me in the room, but the rest was up to me.

I totally understood and expected that. I didn't reach out to him for him to *give* me a job. I reached out to him for an opportunity that I expected would be beneficial to both of us. I killed the audition. I didn't get a lead role. I got the role of LaKeisha Grant, the childhood friend of the main character's wife, Tasha St. Patrick, played by talented Naturi Naughton. My role was small, but I knew it could turn into something bigger.

The show got picked up for a second season, which we are currently filming, and my role has been expanded. I even have my first sex scene in this upcoming season. I took the opportunity to audition and turned it into a growing role on a successful TV series.

Some people would have given up after they tried to reach out to 50 Cent and he didn't respond. I kept reaching out until he did. The power of persistence.

If he didn't answer my text, I would have called or texted him again and said, "I don't mean to be a bug, but I'm just checking in."

Harmless. And at the same time, letting him know I'm not going away until he responds. You need to be persistent without being threatening or heavy-handed.

I think a lot of women have trouble being direct about what they want because they're afraid of seeming pushy. There is a thin line between pest and persistence. You have to keep trying. You may not get what you want at first, but that's okay. The way I see it, you didn't have the job or opportunity anyway. So if you were a pest and blew it, you really didn't lose anything. In fact, you gained something valuable—knowledge. Knowledge about how far to push next time. And we all know that knowledge is power.

If you're going to be persistent, you will probably get the opportunity you're looking for. People look at me and think that because of where I am, I don't have to pursue my goals, that they just come to me. A few more doors are open to me now, for sure, but I still have to push and work to get through.

I've watched the most successful people achieve their goals through this thing called persistence. You can watch *E! True Hollywood Story* over and over again and you hear how this artist or actor kept pushing and knocking on doors until finally someone said yes.

Opportunities can become successes only when we take the initiative to go for it.

Sometimes we miss opportunities simply because we *miss* the opportunity. We don't see it and we don't grab hold of it.

I have a friend, Mo McRae, who is an actor. He played

in *Gridiron Gang* and *The Butler*, and was Tyler on *Sons of Anarchy*. We shot a movie together in 2014, *November Rule*, produced by Queen Latifah and her partner, Shakim Compere.

Mo is a good friend. We speak about three times a week and we talk about everything. It's good to have friends in the business to bounce things off of. During one of our chats he told me he was heading off to Detroit to work on an independent film.

"The script is amazing," Mo told me. "And it's a Tommy Oliver film."

"Tommy Oliver!" I said.

I was excited to hear that it was a Tommy Oliver film. I had a role in his 2013 film, *1982*, starring Hill Harper. It was a great film and it introduced me to the world of independent filmmaking and film festivals. When I hung up from Mo, I texted Tommy.

"Let me find out you don't call me anymore when you're doing movies. Remember, I was one of the first to rock with you. LOL!"

I wanted the message to be lighthearted, but I also wanted it to be clear that I wanted to work with him again.

He texted me back: "La, I assumed you were unavailable because you're doing *Power*."

I had just wrapped the last few scenes of *Power* and I was very available and I told him so.

"You know what?" he said. "I actually have the *perfect* role for you! We start shooting this weekend. It will be a six-day shoot. I'll send you the script. Can you make it?"

Of course!

He e-mailed the script to me and I loved the role. I was playing a thugged-out lesbian, which was a total departure from the roles I was used to getting. I loved it because it would show my range and ability to do something people aren't used to seeing me do. (See Chapter Eleven for more on reinventing yourself.)

But none of this would have happened if I just had a casual conversation with Mo and went on about my business. I got all of the details from him about the film and knew that while it was a small budget, that it would be a solid opportunity for me. I didn't wait for my agent or manager to get involved, which is something many people do. Sometimes you pass along opportunities and people don't follow up with the same fervor you would. It's great to have representatives, but when you have a personal relationship with the filmmaker, it makes a good impression to reach out yourself. It shows how eager you are.

Opportunities sometimes happen in the moment and you have to carpe diem—seize the day!

I didn't let a day go by without reaching out to the director directly. I wasn't overly pushy, but I playfully let him know that I wanted to be a part of what he was doing. That did two things—it validated him, by letting him know how much I respect his work, and it also let him know that I wasn't too big to pick up the phone myself and make it happen. I'm sure that made an impression on him.

And while I won't be getting rich off of this film, it is exactly the kind of role I wanted to round out the plan I have for my career. I was confident that I would bring a lot to this role because I have been studying and preparing all year to take my acting to another level. Wins for everyone!

That's the other thing. If you're going to be persistent, you will probably get the opportunity you're looking for. But in order for that opportunity to turn into success, you must be prepared for it. You should have the skills to do the job. I have been taking acting classes and getting one-on-one coaches to be prepared for any role that comes my way. With that also comes the confidence. I know I'm ready.

Persistence is also about how you process the word "no." You need to develop the wisdom to understand when to accept a "no." Sometimes a "no" really means "not yet." Or that "no" could be the very thing you need to go in another direction that's even better for you.

I've been in a lot of situations where I've been told no, and by accepting the "no" I was freed up for other projects that were a better fit for me in the end.

Before *Power*, I had auditioned for an HBO series produced by Mark Wahlberg, called *Ballers*. It stars The Rock, Dwayne Johnson, and it's about a bunch of retired football players. I was auditioning for the role of the wife of one of the players. Peter Berg, who did *Lone Survivor* and *Battleship*, was directing the first episode.

After my first reading, I got a callback, which is always a great sign. I went back and auditioned again. I got another callback. I read with Omar Benson Miller from *8 Mile*. We did a screen test together, and I killed it. I know I did. Even Omar said to me afterward, "You did an amazing job."

I felt like I did a great job, too, so it was nice getting confirmation. I was waiting for the call to confirm what I already knew. The call came within the week. They said they were going in a different direction. *What?* Everything went perfectly. How could they go in a different direction? They just said that I wasn't the right one. If I wasn't right, why keep bringing me back? I was devastated.

But that's the business. Maybe they wanted someone with brown eyes and I have green eyes. It could be your height. It could be your size—too skinny or too thick. It could be your complexion or your race. There are so many variables that people look at when considering you for a job and most are out of your control. I got so attached to this one project that it really rocked my world for a minute. I was almost having thoughts like, "Why am I doing this?" Have you ever been so sure about something and just knew it would happen, and then it doesn't? It was as if the rug had been pulled out from under me.

But I had to stop and remember to focus on the positives: You read for Mark Wahlberg, and Peter Berg knows who I am. He invited me to the screening of *Lone Survivor*. He liked me and maybe I will have an opportunity to work with both of them in the future.

I was excited by the possibilities of being on an HBO series. I had all of these thoughts about how this opportunity would open so many doors for me. But this "no" opened another door. That's why you never quit. Don't get discouraged. Because you never know.

A few weeks after I was told I would not be on *Ballers*, I got the call that I had been cast in *Power*. You have to believe that what is meant for you is for you. Had I gotten *Ballers*, I wouldn't have taken *Power*. But *Power* was exactly the right opportunity for me. It shoots in New York, where I live. I didn't have to move Kiyan around or do anything crazy.

I later heard through my manager that the casting director from *Ballers* thought I was really good. She validated what I already felt, which I appreciated. (And a note on being gracious: Even when I didn't get the role, the casting director said she would be definitely looking out for me because of how wonderful I was to work with. Casting directors are the gatekeepers for roles in Hollywood. They are the first line of defense. They have to like you for you to even be seen by producers and directors most of the time. If they like you, you will almost always have work.

On the flip side, if you have a bad reputation with them, you can just about forget it unless you're a superstar who gets his or her jobs straight through the producers.)

Being passed over for a position or a role or what you think is the perfect opportunity may be the best thing to happen for you. While my initial role on *Power* was small and I had no idea if the series would even get picked up, it is now bigger and the series is one of the hottest on the Starz network. I didn't quit. I didn't wallow. Sometimes being persistent is just about knowing that you're good and waiting for the opportunities to come to you. Keep pursuing, but don't get discouraged when one or two pass you by.

I am one of the most persistent people I know. I do not take no for an answer. But I believe I do it in a manner that puts people at ease and makes them receptive.

I know quite a few people who want to pursue an opportunity or a career path and they have reached out to the powers that be who can make the decision. And this is what I've heard when I asked how it's going:

"I called them and they didn't call me back!"

"So did you call them again?" I'll ask.

"No, I didn't want to bother them."

"You need them, they don't need you. You need to call or e-mail them until you get an answer!"

Too many of us don't understand the value of being persistent. We feel like we're bothering people or pestering people. I say, it's not what you do, but *how* you do it. You can call someone every day and not be a pest or you can call someone once and be a pest. You have to learn how to be persistent without being annoying.

People in positions of power or decision makers expect people to ask them for opportunities. Most have gatekeepers or barriers protecting them from the general public. But if you're clever enough to figure out how to reach them directly or you have someone make an introduction for you (which is preferred), don't waste the opportunity or the introduction. Map out exactly what you're going to say ahead of time. Role-play. Act out the scene. Put yourself in their position. How would you like to be approached by someone if you held all of the keys?

Ask yourself if someone had to contact you for something, what would be the most effective way that would get you to respond with a yes.

We often don't see people in power as *people*. We put them on a pedestal that's so far out of reach that it's virtually impossible to relate to them. But people are people, just like you and me. Just because they have power and position doesn't mean that they aren't wired just like normal people. They *are* normal people.

You never know why you got rejected. It could be with good reason, and have absolutely nothing to do with you or your talents. In the entertainment industry nowadays they have budget restrictions. A lot of people aren't willing to take a chance on a new or unproven talent—no matter how great they may be. If you have no track record, expect a lot of nos. But eventually someone will say yes and sometimes that's all it takes for everyone else to see your value, too. They almost want someone else to take that chance first.

It may take you stepping away and doing something on your own, focusing on the next opportunity, to entice them to come back around. (That goes for relationships as well as business and work, too.) You do seem way more attractive to people when you're not standing still waiting. No one wants to get on a train that's not moving.

Keeping moving. Keep striving. Don't quit.

CHAPTER SIX
....

The Power of Failing

In my business I fail about ninety percent of the time. If I audition for thirty roles, I may get one or two. I consider that a failure. I went to perform for a job, and I didn't get it. What would you call it? Whether it was within my control or not, I still view it as a failure. Every time I get a call (or in most cases, don't even get the call) that says they went in another direction, I'm sad. I will call one or two friends and vent about it. They will tell me what I already know: "What's for you, you'll get. There's a reason for everything." But it's exactly what I need to hear out loud from someone else, not just in my own head.

Every time I don't get a job, it makes me stronger. It makes me want to do better, and be better. It makes me work harder. So in many ways, my failures are definitely fuel for my success. Failing can be powerful.

When I fail I'm on a mission to make them sorry for not hiring me. I want to make that director or producer say, "Damn! We should have hired her!" That's how I motivate myself.

I also overcome that feeling of failure by seeking out positive messages. I post these positive messages very often on Instagram. Usually, it's just to motivate and inspire myself. Often it's just a reminder to me to not get down.

> *You can't stop the waves, but you can learn to surf.*
>
> —Jon Kabat-Zinn,
> stress-reduction guru

The idea of viewing failure as a wave in the ocean of your life is exactly how I strive to live my life. I don't really see failures in my life because to me it's just a wave that I need to learn how to surf. They're opportunities to learn and grow.

> *You may encounter many defeats, but you must not be defeated. In fact, it may be necessary to encounter the defeats, so you can know who you are, what you can rise from, how you can still come out of it.*
>
> —Maya Angelou

Beloved author Maya Angelou reminds me that failure or defeat may be just what you need to get you to where you need to be or become who it is you were put here to be.

Positive words and messages like these two quotes, and the others throughout the book, inspire me to combat the so-called failures in life that all of us face. I know how important these words are to me so I hope they inspire you, too.

I read a quote by Malcolm Forbes, the publisher of the illustrious *Forbes* magazine: "Failure is success if we learn from it." Yes! And this one, which is anonymous, really inspired me: "The one who falls and gets up is so much stronger than one who never fell." I love these quotes. They help me to appreciate that I'm not alone in this journey toward finding and creating success. Setbacks and so-called failures are a big part of life and through these powerful words, I learn every day to accept them and use them to make myself stronger. You gain your power in how you deal with failure, how you view it, and how you use it to motivate you to continue to push forward.

One of my favorite quotes is from Michael Jordan, who said: "I've missed more than nine thousand shots in my career. I've lost almost three hundred games. Twenty-six times, I've been trusted to take the game-winning shot and missed. I've failed over and over and over again in my life. And that is why I succeed."

Powerful!

That's how I feel. Some people just do give up. But I came too far. And I've come farther in my life than I ever imagined. I might as well keep going and see where I end up, no matter how many times I'm rejected, no matter how many times I fail to reach an immediate goal I may have set for myself.

For some people it's all about achieving their goal and if they don't hit the mark, they've failed. That's not how I see it.

Melo said to me, "You're the only person I know who will have that door closed in your face a hundred times but you'll come knocking one hundred and one times."

Well, that next door may be the one! I've always turned failure and disappointment into motivation to keep trying. Some of it is innate. But I'm driven by wanting to prove to myself that I can make it.

Melo has quite a different view of failure. At this point in his career, he doesn't have a lot of doors close in his face. He doesn't have to chase a lot of things. He turns down way more things than someone in my position because he can. So for him, sometimes, he's not prepared for when things don't work out. He's not so easy with knocking on that next door. Thankfully, very few doors close in his face. That's just not part of his everyday experience.

Hollywood is a different animal. It's a constant grind. You have to constantly sell yourself and tell people why you're the best person for x-y-z project. You have to constantly deal with rejection and failure. You build up a tolerance for it. And if your attitude is right, it makes you stronger.

With Melo, everyone is clawing to have him on their team. It's definitely a blessing to be in that position. But the vast majority of people are where I am—having to chase opportunities and face rejection.

I was telling Melo about the Urban Film Festival and this up-and-coming director that people were buzzing about. I wanted to work with her so I told him that I wanted to meet her. I bugged someone for her contact information and I sent her an e-mail.

He just smiled and said, "Only you, La, only you!"

She might see my e-mail and say, "Who is this?" and totally ignore me. Or she could respond positively. And if I have a fifty-fifty chance of making an impact or being rejected, I'm going to go for it every time. Even if she doesn't jump at the chance to work with me now, I've planted a seed.

Sometimes when you fail it is absolutely for the best.

While I was on the radio, I really wanted to be a rapper. I very seriously wanted a music career and I spent countless hours in the studio producing what I thought were the dopest tracks. I was doing everything I felt I needed to do to get a recording deal. I had a couple of meetings with record labels. Interscope showed interest in signing me but something happened and the deal fell through. I didn't quit, but everything I tried to do to get my music career off the ground was unsuccessful. I had countless songs. I rapped on different mixed tapes with people like Lil' Kim and Remy Ma. I made some amazing connections. But La La the rapper just never took off.

Was I a failed rapper? Absolutely. Was I a failure? Absolutely not.

Looking back, if I wasn't on MTV I would have probably been successful as a rapper. Being there actually worked against me. It was hard for people to see me beyond that space. And I get it.

When Ludacris pursued his rap career, he was on the radio in Atlanta and people knew him, but it was different. He was a rapper on the radio spinning the kind of hip-hop he would eventually produce. He was connected to it and the audience could see it. I was on a national television show every single day. I was seen as someone who interviewed people in the industry, not as one of them.

But I went for it and the process of going for something—even if you don't make it—is powerful. I learned so much about music, about the business, and most important, about myself. Thank goodness it wasn't my only goal. When the rap career didn't take off, I wasn't left with nothing. I thought about quitting MTV and trying for this rap thing full out. But I always wanted to have a backup. Rap was my first love. But it was my backup plan—television—that actually put me in the position to realize so many of my other goals.

I believe in following your dreams wholeheartedly. But I also believe in being realistic and not putting all of your eggs in one basket.

If you "fail" at something, it could just be to prepare you for something else. It could be to change your course or path. Stay positive and see each failure as an opportunity or a possibility.

Five Reasons Failure Makes You Powerful

Fear of failure is rampant in our society. Whether it's a marriage that didn't make it, a job loss, or a mistake that has some negative consequences, we see failure as a reflection of who we are. Well, no one is perfect, and we're all going to experience some sort of failure in our lives. Why pretend? When we're honest about our failures, they provide the springboard for growth. In fact, oftentimes we need to fail in order to learn.

So, let's stop with the shame and pretending everything is perfect. Instead, embrace failure. It's actually good for you.

1. It teaches you about yourself. There's no clearer mirror than facing your fears and disappointment after something

didn't work out the way you wanted it to. Use failed attempts as an opportunity to look inside yourself. Don't spend too much time thinking about what you could have done differently, but do check yourself to see how you can improve for next time. Find the lesson and move on.

2. It shows you what doesn't work. When things don't work out the way you planned, you learn what combination of people, actions, and circumstances don't lead to success. So, now you're one step closer to figuring out what does!

3. It makes you stronger. We've all known some of those people who seem to have life handed to them on a silver platter. Everything seems to go their way without effort. But a funny thing happens to those folks when it all stops being so easy—they fall apart. Their self-worth takes a big hit, and they can crumble. When you power through failure and learn from it, you become stronger and better able to deal with just about anything life throws your way. I think of it as building up my success muscles.

4. It gives you understanding and empathy. The sting of failure makes us less likely to judge other people unfairly. It makes us better able to understand others' struggles and helps us to be more open and kinder because everyone has doubts, fears, and challenges. People who pretend they've never failed at anything are often negative and judgmental

of others, making them less likely to learn and grow from their experiences.

5. It makes you better. Simply put, failure makes you better. You have to face up to your own imperfections and keep going. Doing so takes courage and resolve. We all respect people who persevere in the face of challenges. Failure teaches you that you can get through even the toughest times and come out stronger. What's more powerful than that?

TIME-OUT

Learn to Be by Yourself

You only grow when you are alone.
—Paul Newman

You cannot be truly successful until you know yourself. That means knowing not just what you want out of life, but also what drives you and makes you tick as a person. I've talked in this book about finding your passion. But you cannot possibly know your passion until you know yourself.

How can you know yourself if you can't stand being by yourself?

It is great to have a support system. But you have to learn to be your own best friend. The decisions you make, you will either benefit from or suffer the consequences of. So you have to get to a point where you trust yourself. That means knowing yourself.

You can't really know yourself, what you like, what you don't like, what makes you tick, until you spend some time alone with yourself.

This was perhaps the most difficult power play I've ever had to make in my entire life.

I hate being alone. So much so, that if Kiyan has a sleepover and Melo is on the road, I will get on the phone and invite my cousin or friends to spend the night. If I'm on location for a movie, it is not at all unusual for me to fly out my brother or my cousin Dice to be with me at the hotel while I'm there. I don't like to be alone. Never have. A sadness comes over me when I'm by myself.

But as I get older, I'm understanding the power of one—being alone.

You learn so much about yourself when you're alone. You get to refine things in your character that you can never do with people around. You get to discover things you would never discover otherwise.

Those moments in the mirror staring at yourself or that quiet time in a room with no television, text messages, or distractions is the time when you get to listen to that little voice inside—the one that actually is your compass and guide. You cannot hear that voice if all of your time is spent around people with their chatter and noise.

It's also frightening. Being forced to really look at yourself. How many of us do that? Really dig deep and look at who we are? Are you happy with what you see? I can honestly say that while I have things to work on, for sure, at my core I'm somebody I like. I knew that before I started spending more time with myself. But being alone has given me a greater appreciation and allowed me to grow even more.

The other power in learning to be alone is that you build your internal muscles. People—friends, family members, mentors, teachers, etc.—can be crutches. You can hide behind them or allow them to make decisions on your behalf. Having to stand on your own and stand up for yourself is incredibly empowering.

You can have the people around you, but knowing that you can do it yourself makes all the difference.

CHAPTER SEVEN

Everyone Needs a Good Coach

*What is a teacher? I'll tell you: it isn't someone
who teaches something, but someone who inspires
the student to give of her best in order to discover
what she already knows.*

—Paulo Coelho

*Natural abilities are like natural plants, that
need pruning by study.*

—Sir Francis Bacon

I met TV producer Cris Abrego when I was hosting *Flavor
of Love*. He was the mastermind behind the Celebreality
craze, which included hit reality shows like *The Surreal
Life, Rock of Love, Charm School*, and *Strange Love*. A couple
of years after *Flavor of Love*, he approached me about
doing a reality TV show around my wedding.

I really didn't want to turn my wedding into a spectacle, but Cris assured me that whatever I wanted to show and didn't want to show, they would honor. They would film it the way I wanted. I figured there were some moments that would be helpful for other people getting married and there were some fun elements to the whole process of me getting married that would be entertaining. It wouldn't be one of those drama and mayhem reality shows. It would be just a look at the days and weeks leading up to our big day. So I agreed to do it. It turned out better than I expected.

That wedding show turned into an offer to do my own show, *Full Court Life*, which ended up running for five seasons.

But during those five years I wasn't content to just star in and executive produce my own reality show; I also wanted to learn the other side of the business—the *business* side. I wanted to understand how one bridge connects to another. I told Cris that I wanted to learn the TV business. I wanted to be in the television business, not just be on TV in front of the camera.

He took me under his wing and taught me what it meant to be an executive producer and gave me the opportunity to grow and become a bigger player in the TV business.

I credit Cris Abrego with resurrecting my career. He gave me an opportunity when I didn't even know what I would do next. He opened a lane for me to get back onto television after leaving MTV and taking time off to have my son. To be honest, I had no freaking clue what I was going to do before this.

Cris also coached me. He showed me how the television business worked, answered any question I had. Sometimes in business you find people who hold on to the answers like it's the secret of creation. They don't want to tell anyone anything. Perhaps they feel by telling people how things work, they will somehow lose their position.

So when you find someone willing to help you, it's a blessing.

I also learned from Cris that you could experience a lot of success and become a power player in your field, while still being yourself. Cris, who is now cohead of Endemol North America, sold half of his production company for a reported two hundred million dollars, but you would never know he was worth that much. He is one of the wealthiest people I know and also one of the most humble. He never forgot where he came from. And like me, he was always looking out for family. When he sold his company, his cousin—who had been working with him for years and was an integral part of the success of 51 Minds—became the president. That's looking out. While that was family, Cris didn't just hand his cousin a job. In fact, his cousin had to really prove himself to overcome the stigma that he got the position only because he was Cris's cousin.

He also resurrected the careers of so many people. What was Flavor Flav doing before *The Surreal Life* and then *Flavor of Love*? Brigitte Nielsen? Or Bret Michaels? He gave so many people new life in television. A good coach maximizes the talent around him and gets the most out of them to win.

A good coach also fosters trust. Cris was a man of his word. When he told me he would do something, he always did. Even so, when he approached me about taking the success of my wedding show and turning it into an actual reality show, I was reluctant. But he reassured me and said, "I will never put you in a position to cause you drama or hurt you." I was able to do it on my terms, by my rules. Cris put me in a position to create the show I wanted.

I believed him. I trusted him.

Perhaps the biggest assist Cris gave me was in showing me how to use this platform he was creating for me to build a brand (more on this in Chapter Ten). As you know, I always wanted to be in entertainment, whether on the radio or on TV, or later as an actress and host. He showed me how to use the show to build endorsement relationships and branding deals through the platform of my reality show.

I will never forget what he has done for me.

In 2014, I agreed to host a New Year's Eve special with Pit Bull on FOX. Why? Because Cris Abrego was producing it and he asked me to do it. I value my relationship with him. So I came out of my comfortable family bubble after the holidays and headed to Miami. And I did so happily and committed to making it an amazing experience for the audience.

When *La La's Full Court Life* started gaining popularity, I told VH1 that I wanted a production deal. I learned through Cris that when you have success that's the best time to leverage your power.

Now I'm also producing other shows for the networks because of Cris Abrego's tutelage. He taught me a lot. He invited me to learn under him and taught me how to build my brand behind the camera as well as in front of it. And he taught me how to form my own production company. I'm now bringing scripted and nonscripted ideas to television.

None of this would be possible without help and guidance. Mentors are important. Someone has to help you on your journey; you're not expected to know how to navigate the complicated business world, or whatever industry you're in, when you're first starting out. But help would not have just come to me. I had to ask for it. The biggest power play you can make is asking for help or advice when you need it.

The other power play is to get training to make sure you're prepared for these opportunities that you create for yourself. And one of the best ways to prepare is by seeking out a coach and expert to help you hone your skills.

When I decided I wanted to move beyond reality TV into acting, the one thing that I knew was that I knew nothing about acting. I knew that it was a skill and that I couldn't just memorize a script, jump in front of the camera, and start "acting." While I may have some raw talent, there's so much more to it.

My best reference for this is basketball. There are plenty of players with raw talent, but in order to win you need to train and you need a good coach. Phil Jackson, Pat Riley, Dean Smith, John Wooden, Red Auerbach are some of the best coaches in basketball. While they had great players with names like Michael Jordan, Bill Russell, Kareem Abdul-Jabbar, and Magic Johnson, it was their coaching that people often credit for their multiple championship titles. Great coaching makes the difference.

That goes for the playing field, the workplace, and even life.

Find coaches around you in many different ways, whether it's someone at a high level that you may not know or a celebrity that you can aspire to be like, or choose someone that you can meet and forge a relationship with. Even someone who works in a different field can provide valuable advice if you're asking the right questions.

Who are your mentors? Who are your role models? Who do you talk to about your dreams and goals? Do they help you shape your vision, create a plan and execute it, or are they just there cheerleading as a sounding board?

How to Find a Great Mentor

In the office, you want to find someone with experience who can help you navigate that space and capitalize on the opportunities. Trying to do it on your own is okay, but you can do much better with help.

1. Set clear goals. Consider what you're hoping to learn from a mentor. It may be advice on getting that next promotion from someone more senior in your company or field, or it may be advice on changing jobs or industries from someone in the career path you're trying to break into. Have clear goals so you can ask concrete questions during your conversations.

2. Search outside the box. While a senior level colleague at your company makes a lot of sense as a mentor, don't be afraid to search outside the box. First, consider looking outside of your company through industry networking groups, volunteer organizations, or other activities. Being involved in many different circles will enable you to meet a wide range of people with varying expertise. Networking sites like LinkedIn are also great places to search for people in your area and in your field.

3. Be confident. Approach your potential mentor with confidence and a positive attitude. Describe your current job and aspirations with pride and confidence in your abilities. After all, if you're not confident that you have potential, why would someone want to spend time with you?

4. Have an open mind. After starting the relationship with your mentor, you may immediately get the hand up that you imagined. Don't try to control the conversation too much with one-sided questions about your career and your job. Instead, listen to stories about their experiences and see what you can learn about them. And ultimately, don't be afraid to ask for the specific advice you need.

5. Make it a two-way street. The mentor relationship is naturally one-sided, leaning toward you getting important information from your mentor. But you can still make it a fun and positive experience for both parties. Enjoy your meetings and each other's company. Express your gratitude. And embrace any opportunities you have to share information and educate your mentor on anything you can.

There will come a time when you'll need a helping hand to get to that next level. You will need mentors, supporters, and/or coaches. The best coaches are the ones who make you a better power player.

When I decided I wanted to act, I knew I needed a coach. One of the first things I did was seek out someone who could teach me how to act. I asked around and I kept hearing the name Lesly Kahn. She has an acting school that was close to my house in Los Angeles so I checked it out.

She was really intense. She cursed a lot and she really pushed people's buttons, but I loved it. I knew if I was going to get better, I needed someone who was going to challenge me, not baby me. And Lesly delivered.

After that first class, I decided to enroll in one of her active-intensive programs, which was like a military boot camp for actors. It was six straight hours of training—analyzing scripts, studying scenes, going over techniques and methods—followed by homework. You had partners and you'd have to meet up afterward and work on the things you learned in boot camp.

I was a sponge, soaking up every bit of knowledge Lesly and her team was dishing out. It didn't feel like work at all, even though I was putting in some long hours. But that's what commitment looks like. If you really want to accomplish a goal, you will have to put in the work and train hard to achieve it.

I got to meet a lot of other budding actors, people who had the same goal I had—to become great at acting.

One person I partnered with was an actress named

Xosha Roquemore. I would go to her house to rehearse and she would come to mine. She played Jo Ann in the movie *Precious*, which garnered her a nomination for the Washington DC Area Film Critics Association Award for Best Ensemble in 2009. But she hadn't been able to get much work after that role. She would tell me about her frustrations going on auditions and never getting the roles she was going for. But she didn't quit. She kept working and training. We shared the same work ethic and philosophy: when all else fails, keep working. And Xosha would be in class diligently.

She finally booked a job. She's a regular on FOX's *The Mindy Project*. She plays Tamra, an outspoken, sometimes eccentric nurse at Mindy's office. I'm so happy for her because I know the work she put in to get there. Xosha is super funny and dope and it's great to see the fruits of someone's labor paying off.

When I moved back to New York, I knew I had to find a place to train there, too. I asked Lesly for recommendations and she said Bob Krakower had a great school. I started training with him and came to find out a lot of people I knew were also being coached by Bob Krakower, including Omari Hardwick, who stars in *Power*.

I also needed some more personalized coaching, especially when I'm prepping for a big role or audition, or traveling to a movie set. Lesly connected me with one of her teachers, Kristina Sexton, who is now my personal coach (and who has grown into one of my best friends). When I need one-on-one attention she will come to my house and work with me on an audition or a particular scene. She will even fly out to wherever I am if I'm working on the set of a movie.

Having a coach—a good coach—is invaluable.

Even in the gym, a trainer is important. That person will push you so much farther than you will ever push yourself.

Real power understands how to plug into the power of others. Understanding the need for a coach, a teacher, or a mentor makes you a power player.

You can also learn from watching.

One of my biggest mentors when I first started my radio career was Chaka Zulu. But I also learned by simply watching the morning talk show host Ryan Cameron. I would hang out after my overnight shift and help him with his show. I would pull the songs for his show, which used to be a major process before modern technology made everything digital. And while I know he appreciated the help, I was gaining so much knowledge watching him. I saw how he went to breaks, how he handled callers, what he did in preparing for each show. Sometimes being a help to someone else can be a tremendous help to you.

I became immersed in radio. I would sit in my car and listen to shows I loved and I would keep a notebook and jot down segments that I thought were really cool. There was one afternoon drive show that would play new music and have the audience rate it, Pan it or Play it. I thought that was so cool because it got the audience involved in a way that empowered them.

I incorporated a similar segment when I was hired in Los Angeles.

In Atlanta there was also a woman who worked on Ryan Cameron's show who was a passive mentor to me. Her name was Eboni Elektra and she did gossip on his show. While she did gossip, it was always classy, never bashing or trying to destroy people. I learned from her that you could do something like gossip in a way that wasn't dirty or grimy. She never burned bridges and I noticed whenever an artist or celebrity came to the station they looked for Eboni Elektra. Everyone loved her.

I took a lot of notes watching Eboni Elektra. I also loved the way she carried herself. She always dressed fly. She was just a great role model.

Finding the right role model for you is just like dating—you need to have the right chemistry and values. If you want different things or have different visions at the end of the day, it just won't work. Be selective about the relationships you invest in, especially professionally. You'll be spending a lot of time and energy creating a solid and mutually beneficial relationship, so it's important to select a mentor that's right for you.

Here are some factors to consider when selecting a coach or mentor.

- Get references. Make sure you ask several people you trust about the person you're considering working with. Credentials are great, but there's nothing like eyewitnesses to get a full picture of what you can expect.

- Make sure the personalities match. My acting coach is intense, she curses, she's tough. But that's exactly what I need. Maybe that personality wouldn't work for someone else. You have to know yourself and find a coach who can get the best out of you.

- Know when it's time to move on. You may need several coaches to take you to the next level. Don't be stuck with one person. As you grow, challenge yourself. There are some coaches who are great for beginners and others who are great with veterans. Be mindful of where you are and if you're no longer learning, be prepared to move on.

Selecting the right mentor or coach can be the difference between winning and losing. A bad coach can derail your plans. A good coach will bring out the best in you and ensure that you have the tools, mind-set, and foundation to win.

CHAPTER EIGHT

....

Training Camp

I hated every minute of training, but I said, "Don't quit. Suffer now and live the rest of your life as a champion."

—Muhammad Ali

Luck has nothing to do with it, because I have spent many, many hours, countless hours, on the court working for my one moment in time, not knowing when it would come.

—Serena Williams

I was offered an exciting and challenging role in a movie. The call came in on a Monday, and I had to be in Detroit by Friday for six days. I had an audition back in New York the following Monday. Before leaving for Detroit, I got an acting class in. I wanted to make sure I was ready. The role was a departure from what I was used to playing, and I wanted to make sure I was ready.

While I was in Detroit, I called my personal acting coach and asked her if she had any time during that week to get me ready for the role for which I was going to audition. I had a bunch of frequent-flier miles and I flew her out for a couple of days to work with me in between my tapings for the movie.

One of the actors I know said, "Tell me what you love about acting."

I told him, "I love the challenge. I love the work I have to put in to get better. And I love seeing the work pay off."

I have to work so hard because acting doesn't come as naturally to me as radio and television did. I was a natural on the radio. Once that mic was turned on, I owned that space. And while I definitely worked hard, I knew I didn't have to work as hard as some others. Working on television was also natural. My timing, my comfort in front of the camera, just knowing how to be myself without being nervous or overdoing it, was a gift that I had. It was all very easy for me.

Acting has been quite a different game. I had to train. I had to go to school. And I'm not alone. In my acting classes are actors who are very accomplished. There are people you would see in movies and on television all of the time. There are people who have won awards. Yet they are there all of the time.

Friends and colleagues for whom acting comes more easily tell me they still have to put in the work. They may not have to put in the eight hours that I do, but to be great, they tell me, even they still have to put in their time. They still have to train.

I was at a film festival in 2013 for a film, *1982*, that I did with Hill Harper. There was another film at the festival that everyone was buzzing about, *12 Years a Slave*. We were among the first people to see a screening of this film and I remember sitting in my seat afterward not moving. I had to soak it all in. It was a lot to take in. All of the performances were incredible, but one in particular just jumped off the screen.

When I got home, I had to research Lupita Nyong'o. I needed to know who she was, and where she came from, I was so impressed. I felt like I had discovered a great secret. We all did, because we talked about the performances after the screening.

I later watched with pride as Lupita Nyong'o walked up on that stage for the 2014 Oscars and grabbed that gold statue for appearing in her very first feature film, *12 Years a Slave*. I felt like I had known something before everyone else.

She was an overnight sensation, many people will say.

She not only won an Academy Award for Best Supporting Actress for her portrayal of Patsey, she also won twenty other awards for her performance in *12 Years*, including the Screen Actors Guild Award and an MTV Movie Award for Best Female Performance.

But Lupita didn't just come out of nowhere. She spent many, many years training both in America and overseas, including in Kenya, where she starred on television shows and wrote, produced, and directed a documentary and a couple of music videos.

When she wanted to take her career to the next level, she enrolled in Yale School of Drama. She must have worked very hard and performed well there because the year she graduated, she won the Herschel Williams Prize, awarded to students with "outstanding ability." I know all of this from my research.

But with all of Lupita's abilities, she still felt she needed training. In fact, during an interview she was asked how she was able to tap into the raw emotions of playing Patsey. She said, "Training helps, for sure. I don't know if I could have done Patsey without that technical training, tools to get me there every day."

Behind every success story, there is usually a story of hard work and training that led to that success.

It is very rare for someone to be great out of the box. They call that beginner's luck. As I learned reading *The Alchemist* by Paulo Coelho—an acclaimed and truly inspiring novel that I highly recommend—beginner's luck can happen only once. You have just one breakout moment in your life. But sustained success—real greatness—comes over time with putting the work in.

That goes for acting and it certainly goes for being in physical shape. Everybody I know wants a nice body. While there are all sorts of surgical procedures to suck out fat and move things around to get the shape you want, the best bodies I've ever seen have been the ones where people put the work in to get it.

And here's a secret: Even those who go the surgical route *still* have to work out and train to maintain all of the work they paid for to look good. If you get all of that work done and you don't work out, you will end up back to square one. At the end of the day, there is no escaping hard work and training.

In my increased role on *Power*, they told me I would be doing a sex scene where I'd be showing a lot of skin. So guess what. I had to hit the gym consistently to get camera-ready and in love-scene shape.

I don't ever want that to be a reason why I don't get a job. If I don't get a job, I don't want it to be because I didn't put the work in.

There is a strong connection between physical training and professional training. I see it most in my capacity as an actress, where your appearance can be everything. But it's deeper than that. My acting coach tells us all of the time that our day should consist of acting classes, going to the gym, and eating right.

"That's your job," she says. "It's all part of the program."

Actor and singer Tyrese often says that how a person treats their body is how they really feel about themselves inside. I don't necessarily agree with this, but I do know that being in shape can give you an advantage.

Training, both physical and mental, is a regular part of my day.

I just started something entirely new December 1, 2014: doing things consistently. I have been very sporadic in my life. I will go so hard on a lot of things, usually whatever I'm currently working on, burn myself out, and then do nothing for long stretches. Then I stress out when I need to get ready for the next role or event, which starts in a few weeks. I cram and hit the gym to get back into shape.

It's a vicious cycle that I committed myself to stopping on December 1. Instead, I work out consistently, doing a little something daily so that I'm *always* ready. Before, I would self-sabotage. I wouldn't work out for a while. Then a job would come up and I would be in overdrive again. It's literally the craziest thing ever. And it had to stop.

Now I've taken up boxing—something I discovered a couple of years ago and I absolutely love. I can box every day without feeling overwhelmed and crazy because I love it. But boxing alone won't give me the kind of tone I like, so I also incorporate weights. With the boxing, I'm jumping rope, which is great for cardio. I like the results, so that keeps me motivated. So far, so good.

The consistency I'm building with my workouts I also carry over into my career, especially with acting. Instead of taking classes or calling a coach only when I'm prepping for a new role or audition, I make it part of my regular routine so I'm always improving and challenging myself.

I get up at seven most mornings and get Kiyan ready for school. I take him to school and when I'm preparing for a role, I head to acting class after dropping him off. I will grab some breakfast and make sure I'm on time for the nine a.m. class.

I'm always excited to go to acting class because I never know what I'll learn or who I'll meet. My class is full of actors who are working in television, commercials, movies, and on Broadway. The man who plays Mufasa in *The Lion King* on Broadway was in one of my classes. Here was someone who is accomplished and successful and awesome, but he still takes classes. It always encourages me to see respected, working actors in class striving to get better and perfecting their craft. It's a trait that I have—never rest on your laurels.

During our eight hours in acting class, we watch scenes and break them down in groups. We will do some improvisation and critique one another. We will take a break and then come back and break down more scenes

and work on different techniques. I'm like a sponge in acting class, absorbing as much as I can. Time flies while I'm
in class. It's over around five thirty or six and then I'm
home and back to being wife and mom.

I make the sacrifice to take acting classes two times a
week because I'm determined to be the best I can as an
actress.

There are a million things I can do besides acting
class. I can make a lot of excuses for why I don't need to go.
But I go because I have seen the results of working hard.

Training and preparation are usually tedious, boring,
and hard. Most of us don't want to do it. And when we're
doing it, we want to quit. I know that's true for me—especially when it comes to going to the gym and sometimes
even acting class. It's a lot of hours. But I talk to myself
before I go. I get my attitude right because doing something you need to do with a bad attitude will not help you
get the most out of the situation. Going there complaining
and with a Debbie Downer demeanor will ruin the whole
experience—not just for you, but for those around you because your attitude is contagious. Good or bad.

So I give myself a pep talk. I get revved up and I tell
myself all of the wonderful benefits I'm going to get out of
this class. I tell myself how much I'm going to learn and
grow and how I will have an advantage next time, how
much more confidence it will give me.

Instead of saying what I might say like, "This is bullshit," or "Some of the best actors never take acting classes!" I play mind games with myself. I make it fun. I challenge myself. I tell myself how this class is going to give me an edge. I get myself excited about learning new things.

It's a dog-eat-dog world—so many industries and career paths are highly competitive, especially in Hollywood. There is so much competition. You have to give yourself every edge you can. Training is the thing that can separate you from the pack. So you have to ask yourself: Do I want it bad enough? Do you want that job? Do you want that nice body? Do you want to start that business? Well, you will have to study, train, and work hard to get it!

And yes, it will be hard. If it was easy everyone would be doing it. You have to push through the hard parts. Find a way.

In addition to taking classes, another way that I train is by watching others. I was recently filming a movie with the fabulous Hill Harper. He is un-freaking-believable and I don't believe he gets his proper due as one of the best actors of our generation. Check out his film *The Visit*, where he plays a man with AIDS. It will blow you away.

So when I had the opportunity to actually be in a movie with him, I was thrilled. I would get to see him perform up close. I would also be able to ask him questions. I watched him work several times just to see his technique, how he handled various scenes and his pacing. Even when we weren't in scenes together, I stood on the sidelines and watched him work. I took notes because part of training is being a good student.

Afterward I asked him who coached him because you don't get that good without someone helping you. I had no shame in asking because I always believed that a closed mouth doesn't get fed. Some people in our business don't want to share information. They somehow feel that by giving you help it will take something away from *them*. I will always ask anyway. I'm not afraid of no. And I also don't live like that. I will always give help when asked and Hill Harper didn't hesitate to not only tell me where he trained, but he also gave me some pointers for my next scenes.

I'm constantly trying to add weapons to my repertoire. I'm always in training/learning mode.

Training gives you the confidence to know whether you're ready or not. I auditioned for a role recently and when my manager saw the tape of the audition, she said, "I have to be honest, I don't love it." She felt that I seemed a little too angry. I looked at it again and it was exactly the kind of performance I went in to do.

I totally respect the opinion of my manager, but I also know what it is I'm trying to achieve. I have prepared and trained to get to a certain place. And this performance was the one I set out to give.

After looking at the piece again, I called my manager and said, "I think you're being a hard critic. This is a great tape." The next day she said she thought about it and I was right.

I didn't get the job. But I am still confident in what I put on that tape because I had trained to put in just that performance. I was confident because of my training—confident enough to go against what my manager was telling me and confident enough to stand by my feelings about it. I had to look at her opinion as just that—one person's opinion. I knew I killed the audition. If I felt good about it, then that's all that matters.

Being trained makes you prepared, which allows you to try different things, stretch yourself. Training gives you freedom.

CHAPTER NINE

The Uniform: Dress for Success

Clothes are never a frivolity: they always mean something.

—James Laver, art and fashion historian

I have never really worked a nine-to-five job in my entire life. Nobody taught me the dos and don'ts of appropriate dress. I learned by watching and listening. Working at the radio station at night, I would always be in baggy jeans and a sweatshirt, sneakers, very casual gear. I remember our first staff meeting during the day. I showed up wearing what I normally wore, but I looked around the room and saw the executives and sales reps that I never got to see because they would all be gone by the time I showed up to work.

It didn't take me but a minute to realize that I wasn't

dressed appropriately for a staff meeting. Nobody said anything to me but at the next staff meeting I had on a pair of black slacks, a blazer, and shoes. I naturally made the adjustment and I'm sure it was refreshing for people to see my versatility.

I was always a good student of people. I watched and learned and took heed.

When I was interning at the radio station, I would see women show up to interview for advertising, sales, or secretarial positions and many didn't have a clue about how to present themselves. I would hear the staff talking about the candidate and it wasn't pretty.

"Look at that chick in the lobby!" someone would say.

I'd go out to the waiting room and see a young woman wearing a way-too-short skirt with a blouse unbuttoned so low that it was exposing all of her breasts. Her outfit was capped off with some thigh-high boots. Now that outfit might be cool for an evening out on the town on a date or hanging with your girls, but it was a no-go for a job interview. Nobody said anything to her. But there would be a lot of comments made *about* her.

"I wonder what position she's interviewing for?" another one of our deejays would say. "Missionary? She looks like she came here straight from the club, yo!"

I paid attention to that. These guys would definitely date her or ask her out, but they didn't take her seriously as a professional. It was no surprise that she did not get the job. She might have been highly qualified, but she didn't know the first rule: Dress for success.

To some, focusing on your clothing may seem superficial. Of course, we should be judged by the work we do, our talents, gifts, and work ethic. We should be judged by how good we are as people. But our presentation is the very first thing people use to determine our value. It's the first hurdle we have to cross before it is decided if we're worthy to go to the next level. It's just the way it is. It's one of the unspoken rules of the game. People may never say that the reason you didn't get that job or promotion was because you weren't dressed in accordance with the standards set for that particular position. But I'm telling you now that could be the reason.

Conforming may not be your thing. Cool. Then perhaps you should find a career where you can wear whatever you like. Or perhaps you can be your own boss, start your own business where you can walk around like Steve Jobs did every day in a black mock turtleneck and a pair of jeans and sneakers.

But how likely is that? I see so many people who want to march to their own beat and show how much of an individual they are.

I have friends who try to buck the system. "I want to be who I am. And I should be judged on my merits!"

If you don't want anyone to change you, fine. You won't have a job. There aren't many jobs—even the coolest job—that will tell you to dress however you want. Even those dress-down Fridays have parameters and rules because they know people will go too far.

Once you're on the job for a while and people get to know you and love you for who you are, perhaps you can slip into your own style a bit. But you will never get that far if you don't first impress them with the only thing they can judge you by when first meeting you. You want to get to the point where they want to know you, when you can let your hair down and be more of yourself, perhaps.

It doesn't mean a turtleneck and trousers everywhere you go. What's appropriate for an MTV meeting is different from a meeting at NBC. MTV is music and you can be trendy and cool. At NBC you're sitting with older, more corporate people.

To me dressing for success and making sure your look is appropriate is more common sense than anything. People see me as a glamour girl. But I'm really a tomboy. I totally prefer to be in some sweats or jeans and sneakers with no makeup. That's how I'm most comfortable. But when it's time to dress, I know what I need to do. You have to be prepared and flexible enough to be able to dress for success whenever you need to.

Make sure you're appropriate.

Let's say your aspiration is to be a makeup artist. Then

you better beat the hell out of your face when going for that job because that's appropriate for that job. Your face will be your audition. But what's the norm in your field of interest? What do people usually do in that profession?

Every office and every workplace has a dress code or uniform. Even Starbucks didn't allow people to show tattoos if they had them until recently and still with restrictions. You should never be a distraction from what you're promoting or selling, which is your company's goods and services, or sometimes yourself.

If you have dreadlocks or natural hair, you can wear it in such a way that it is appropriate for your job. It's not selling out to pull it back in a neat bun. It's making sure you do everything in your power to secure the job. I have seen the nicest natural hairstyles. Your hair doesn't have to look like you haven't combed it in twenty days. You don't need a weave and a perm, or hair extensions to look nice. What you need to look like is that you care about your appearance. What your appearance must say to anyone looking is: "You're important enough for me to take that extra time."

I live by that philosophy. If I'm trying to make an impression on someone, I take care with what I wear.

I recently had a casual meeting with a director. I could have worn sweats or dressed down. But I put on a pair of jeans and I threw on a crisp white shirt and a blazer. It was casual, and simple. But it also showed care. Even if they said, "I see you're dressed up today," it shows they noticed that they were important enough for me to take the time to dress up for them.

Before I meet anyone, I try to find out about him or her. I want to know who I'm meeting. Have they ever met me before? All of those factors play into what I will wear.

I would rather be dressed properly than underdressed. No one will knock you for dressing well. And showing you put some effort and thought into your outfit might just secure you a job.

First and foremost, you need to read the situation. Consider who will be there, where it will be held, and what the expectations are. While I subscribe to the rule that it's better to be overdressed than underdressed, there are also times when keeping it simple is the best play. For example, I decided to attend the 2014 Urban Film Festival in New York City. *Beyond the Lights*, starring Gugu Mbatha-Raw and Nate Parker, opened the festival. I was looking forward to seeing the film, which I had heard so many great things about, but I was really dying to meet the director, Gina Prince-Bythewood. She had directed one of my favorite films of all time, *Love & Basketball*, which was basically the story of my life. She is someone I have always wanted to work with and I wanted to let her know how much I admire what she does.

I spent quite a bit of time in my closet looking for the right outfit. There would be a red carpet event, and I wanted to look nice, but not too nice. A lot of times, people try to steal the show or upstage other people on the red carpet. (People do this in real life too . . . trying too hard.) That's okay to do if it's your event or film. But if it's not, you should dress well, but you shouldn't try to do too much with your outfit. I also wanted something that would show me as a serious actress. That's a power play.

How you dress makes a big statement about who you are. True power players understand how to use their wardrobe to send a message.

For me on this day, I wanted to make a connection. I didn't want anyone distracted by what I was wearing. I didn't want to turn up on the front pages of the blogs, upstaging the stars of the event. I wanted to fly under the radar as someone in the industry there to support.

I selected a short, above-the-knee dress. It said young, fun Hollywood, but also demure. When I walked up to Gina Prince-Bythewood and introduced myself I wanted her to be able to see me in any role she may have had available. I wanted her to say to herself, "Yes, I can see her being educated *and* sexy."

The easiest way to prevent yourself from being typecast is to not be *type-castable*. Show you can be versatile.

That goes for the office as well. You want to create the image that you want for yourself. How you dress is the easiest way to get people to see you the way you want to be seen.

Every woman should have these basic items in her wardrobe to build polished and professional looks by pairing with accessories:

- A basic black dress (one that can be worn to the office under a blazer)

- A fitted blazer, a pair of black slacks

- A pair of fitted jeans (that will look nice with a blazer)

- A tank top or shell (I suggest a black one and a white one to start)

- Perfect black pumps that are closed toe and comfortable enough to be on your feet all day.

With those items you can mix and match and pretty much be appropriate for any occasion. You can throw on a different scarf or shoes and have new looks just about every day. For men, it's even easier to dress well. But every man should have a nice, well-fitted suit in his wardrobe and a nice blazer that can be thrown over khakis or jeans. A couple of button-down shirts and some basic ties can round out a professional look for any man.

Think out of the box and be creative when obtaining these items. You don't need to spend a whole lot of money to have the right look. There are thrift stores that have high-end and nice items for less. There are clearance sales and even stores like Forever 21 and Century 21 where you can get nice outfits and workplace-appropriate gear. You don't have to go to Barneys and Neiman Marcus. But if you do shop there, go when there are ridiculous sales and comb the clearance racks. You can look great for a little amount of money. I know someone who needed a suit for an audition, and couldn't afford a nice one. So they went online and rented one for a day. You can even borrow clothes.

If you don't have any money and are coming through hard times, there are organizations like Dress for Success (dressforsuccess.org) that will not only provide you with an outfit to go on your job interview, but also work with you on your interviewing skills—what to say and what not to say.

When I was younger and I had job interviews and auditions and I had no "professional clothes," I would ask my mom if I could borrow a blazer. It's okay to borrow clothes until you get the job and can afford your own. Do not go into debt to have the right outfit. In fact, I would wait until I built up savings before even buying new clothes.

I know someone who just got a job selling Tom Ford perfume. She was so excited that she went out and got a Tom Ford outfit. But it was the only one left. There was only one suit left and it wasn't her size and it was ill fitting.

So while she had on a very expensive suit (which she really couldn't afford), it didn't look good on her.

"I don't even own a Tom Ford suit," I said.

I told her to take it back. She could get the Tom Ford blazer, but she had to get it altered and replace the slacks with some less expensive (*much* less expensive) brand. You have to learn to mix and match. Fake it until you make it.

Some people are a slave to labels. But if you're going to wear designer labels, even that has to be done with class. You can't wear it just to wear it. And if it doesn't fit you or your style, don't do it just because it's the hottest thing right now. In fact, classics are your best bets in an office— not the trends.

I also believe you should dress for the job you want, not the one you have. If you want a promotion to a manager's position, you need to start dressing and carrying yourself like a manager.

Pay attention to the power players in your office. See who is getting promoted and look at how they're dressing and follow suit. Literally. People judge you by your appearance. As much as we say it's not fair. That's the truth. If you want to be taken seriously, you have to look the part.

As important as what you wear on your body, it is equally important what you do with your face. There are a lot of makeup trends—thicker eyebrows, ridiculously long false eyelashes, etc. Again, don't follow trends. I would keep it classic and keep it simple.

When you're on your own time you can go crazy with the makeup, the lashes, and the over-the-top lipstick colors. Leave that for your weekends or your private time, and special occasions.

But for the office or day to day, I say keep it simple.

I always keep it simple when I'm not on the red carpet or going to an event. I keep it simple primarily because I'm not that good at applying makeup. Thank goodness, you don't need to be very skilled to pull off a nice, classic look. Less is more—a light-colored lip, mascara, eyeliner. You can't go wrong with that. If you need a light cover-up for marks, do that. But don't overdo it. If you have acne or pimples, covering it with thick makeup really only brings more attention to your problem areas. And going crazy with the colorful eye shadows and the over-the-top lip colors just says that you're trying too hard.

Keep it simple and also keep it appropriate. Take your cues from what's going on in the field you want to pursue.

In my field, sometimes I have to be trendy—but that's what is appropriate. I research movie premieres and award-show red carpets to see the latest trends in beauty. There's this whole minimalist movement right now, focusing on natural beauty and barely there makeup. Look at Zoe Saldana on the red carpet. Simple, not overdone, and yet drop-dead gorgeous. Look at the Oscars or the Golden Globe Awards. Hardly anyone is wearing that heavy makeup.

Sometimes women go too far with trying to be sexy. Again, there's a time and a place to be sexy. Sex appeal, for me, is not what you wear, but rather it's *how* you wear what you wear. Sex appeal is who you are; it comes from within. Too often people equate sexy with the exterior—the cleavage, the cut-out stomach, showing the midriff, the slits in the skirt way up to there.

I was at an audition for a female police officer and someone showed up in a low-cut shirt with her boobs hanging out. Now what kind of cop was she trying to be? I guess she was showing she could be a sexy cop. The role didn't call for that and she didn't get the part.

One of the sexiest women I've ever seen is Angelina Jolie. Sure, she had that one outfit with such a high slit that her entire leg was visible. But, if you go back and look at her on the red carpet, her outfits are really pretty simple. *She's* sexy. She has the confidence to stand out on her own instead of letting her clothes do the talking.

Your swag makes you sexy. You don't need to go overboard with your outfit.

Even when dating, you have to think about what message you're sending.

I've heard women say, "I don't want this guy to think I just want to have sex with him!" But she shows up wearing the smallest top and the tightest skirt, showing all of her goodies. She's sending mixed messages. Her mouth is saying, "I'm not that kind of girl." But her outfit is saying just the opposite. The way you dress should be consistent with who you are in your personal life. You are your own calling card. But in business, adhere to the uniform of that industry.

I learned from a professional stylist the best style tip ever: No matter what you're doing, highlight one thing that you love about yourself. But keep it limited to just the one feature. If it's your legs, wear a skirt or dress above the knee. Don't try to showcase too many things or do too many things at once with your outfit. If you're going to show off your arms, you don't need a slit up the thigh, and a plunging neckline, too. If I'm wearing a skirt above the knees to highlight my legs, I keep the rest of my outfit simple and more modest.

You want whoever is looking to hire you to focus on your credentials, not be distracted by your outfit. It's amazing to me how many people don't understand this.

When Melo was looking for an assistant several years ago, I was helping with the interview process because who knows what he needs better than I do? A lot of people didn't get the job because of their appearance. The job may seem like you're just hanging out with a ballplayer, which sounds like fun. But Melo's assistant would be representing him and me. In our house and outside of our house.

Some of the people who were passed over were highly qualified. But they showed up acting like the job would be all fun and games. I read through all of that just by appearance. Girls were showing up in jeans and T-shirts, graphic tees. This is an assistant position to one of the biggest basketball players in the world and you show up in a T-shirt? His assistant would have to display that they could handle business.

One girl showed up in super-tight body dress. Really? What she was telling me was that she was either there to be around Melo or to meet one of his basketball friends. She wasn't there to be his assistant. But talking to her, she was very professional. It was confusing. Her outfit didn't represent who she was at all. But who's going to sift through that to find out? Not many.

If you're lucky, someone will pull you to the side and say, "You were good and we will bring you back, but next time I want your attire to be different." But that hardly ever happens!

Melo ended up going with a young lady who came to the interview dressed in slacks, a shell, and a black blazer. In our world, that's the uniform for a position like that. Slacks or jeans, a black tank, and a blazer and a nice pump.

As long as you have on that blazer, you're good. When I go in for auditions for the role of an assistant that's what I pull out of my closet.

Her credentials were impeccable and she came highly recommended. She also knew what she was talking about. Perhaps one of the others might have had even better credentials. But she knew how to present and carry herself and that made the difference.

Assistants usually have a high turnover rate. People run through them like water. But she's still working with Melo to this day.

I have a niece who was asking me for help finding a job. She is in the nursing field, and I discovered that jobs are tight in just about every field. Everyone is looking for a job it seems these days. Opportunities are few and far between. My niece has a nursing degree, and she's struggling to find a job. She's having a hard time just getting called in for an interview. So we are working on her presentation. She has to distinguish herself.

If you're in a competitive field, why limit yourself? Why allow someone to disqualify you over something you can totally control—your appearance and presentation.

Dress well and present yourself properly and see if more opportunities don't come your way.

CHAPTER TEN

The Power of Your Brand

I don't want to do anything and everything. I want to be a brand that, every time I leverage my name, I want people to feel sure that it's going to be something good—so whether it be my movies, my perfume, my restaurant, my musical, it'll be good work, good food, and good everything.

—Shilpa Shetty

Social media has given just about everyone a brand. Everything you post on Twitter, FB, Instagram defines you and can either establish you or destroy you. Everyone has to think about how they want to be perceived today.

I know that before hiring people, managers and executives check candidates' social media pages. According to a recent survey, seventy percent of human resources workers admitted to checking the social media activity of a potential hire and rejecting them based on their "Internet behavior."

People must be careful about posting inflammatory or insensitive remarks on Twitter, like the PR rep for the massive digital company IAC who boarded a plane to Africa and decided to tweet: "Going to Africa. I hope I don't get AIDS. Just kidding. I'm white!" She shut off her phone and by the time she landed, she was trending and her entire career had blown up. And she was fired. I bet she wishes she had thought that one out. That's how important it is that you watch what you post—right down to your pictures. Don't be the person who overshares. No one needs to see every public display of affection between you and your significant other. In fact, it can be a turnoff. You must know that some things are better left unseen. Keep some of who you are to yourself. Don't put it all out there; it doesn't help your brand to give too much.

Being a brand means thinking about how you want to be perceived and how you want to be treated. It requires that you look beyond the right now and look a bit into the future. It requires that you ask yourself, "Should I post this selfie of me getting drunk with my friends?" or "Will this video of me making fun of people be perceived well?" "Do I need to put every family photo on my Facebook page?"

That's your brand. And while you can change the ways other perceive you (see Chapter Eleven to learn more about reinventing yourself), that may take much longer than you expect. In the meantime, how many jobs and opportunities will you miss because you didn't make your brand—which is really your good name and image—a priority?

When I was coming up, having a brand wasn't even a thought. It wasn't until after I left MTV and was actually out there trying to reestablish myself that the notion of what my brand should be even came into existence.

After hosting so many reality show reunions, I never thought I would actually do a reality show myself. I simply was planning a wedding when Cris Abrego approached me about filming it for TV. And I thought, Why not?

It turned out to be really a cool experience. I didn't feel violated, and I got comfortable with the reality space. That led to Cris approaching me about doing an actual reality show, following my life. At this point I trusted the folks from 51 Minds and I saw the power that it could have in helping me build and control my brand.

My show was one of the few reality shows on the air that wasn't negative. Later, I would hear people say, "I want to do a reality show like *La La's Full Court Life*." It became the model for how to take a peek into someone's life without it being too intrusive and destructive. Mine was a show that didn't thrive on destructive drama. It was fun and funny. It wasn't about fighting or knocking each other down.

It was refreshing to do a show without having to have all of that stuff. T.I. and Tiny's reality show, *The Family Hustle*, was modeled after mine. It's also produced by 51 Minds. It's a family-friendly, fun show that's now done more than ninety episodes.

We were able to show people that you don't need all of the negativity to make it work. We opened that lane up.

Positivity became part of my brand. Folks in the industry knew I could bring in ratings without fighting, pulling hair, and other ridiculous things. That's really how my career went. That was the La La brand.

Everything I do I have to think, "Does this fit with my brand?" It's not just about taking wholesome roles, but it's also about doing the unexpected. I wouldn't consider myself wholesome (because I'm known to swear and the kinds of things I talk about with my friends are often not G-rated). But by most standards my brand is wholesome. I'm the girl next door, the bestie you can trust. I'm the down-to-earth chick. I also am working on expanding my brand in film to include much more.

When building your brand, you have to start from a place of authenticity. You have to start with who you really are and what you're about and go from there.

My brand had to be honest and drama free because that's who I am. If I tried to do anything else, I'd fail. It's why I'm able to succeed in a space that thrives on drama by not bringing any drama. Because that's not who I am. And people who follow me or who like what I do know what to expect. They know La La is going to be La La.

You have to see yourself as a brand, no matter what field you're in. Your good name and reputation should be important to you whether you're a successful entertainer, a teacher, a plumber, or a housewife. Every single one of us is a brand. If you have a social media handle, you have a brand. If you're out there posting anything or giving your opinion that everyone can read from now until eternity, you have a brand. Shape it, protect it, and make sure it is representing who you really are (or who you want people to believe you are).

There was a story about an elementary school teacher in 2014 who went on Facebook and ridiculed one of her students by name. I'm sure she thought she was speaking just to her close friends and family members. But everything is public. Nothing is private once you post it to a site like Facebook, Twitter, Instagram, or Tumblr. It somehow ended up going viral and it got back to her school and the administration, and it jeopardized her entire career.

She might have been a fantastic teacher in the classroom, but her actions off hours on social media painted her brand in an entirely different way. She lost her power with a few cavalier words spread on social media. She wasn't thinking about her brand and how those words would be perceived.

I operate from a mentality that everyone is paying attention to everything I'm saying and doing at all times. So I have to represent myself in ways that are consistent with my brand.

I didn't realize the power of a brand until after I left MTV. During the radio and MTV stage of my career it was more about having a job to pay my bills or challenging myself to see how far I could take the radio or TV thing.

I had really cool *jobs*. That's how I saw it. I wasn't thinking about much else beyond doing my job and getting my paycheck.

After MTV, I started hearing the word "brand" more frequently. What happened after I left MTV was that I no longer had the security of a steady job. I would get gigs here and there. When they were over, I'd have to get back out there and find work again.

I knew I had to create opportunities for myself. This is where brand building came into play.

It was scary for me at first because I didn't have a safety net. I could have a bad day on the radio or a so-so performance on MTV and I didn't feel as if I would lose my spot. If I performed poorly hosting a reality show re-union, they might never invite me back for another shot. The stakes are much higher when you don't have a safety net. You're just out there.

Beyond performing well, if you don't brand yourself properly, you could find yourself without a career. I was also scared when I left MTV because it was drilled into my head that people failed miserably after MTV. It was called the MTV curse. Veejays and other hosts who would be household names on MTV would never be heard from again when their ride was over.

MTV would even do these "Where Are They Now?" shows and I really got to see how many people actually suffered from this so-called curse. I just knew that I didn't want to be one of those people.

During this time, the opportunities were limited in unscripted television. There weren't many reality shows beyond *The Real World* and *The Osbournes*. There were no reunion shows. There weren't competition shows that needed hosts. It was a completely different time on television! So leaving MTV was very scary to me. Branding? There weren't many outlets to that either, outside of having a high-powered publicist. There was no Twitter or Instagram back them—which are major components to building a brand today.

Today if you're a celebrity you can make money based strictly on how many Twitter and Instagram followers you have. Actually, I know regular people who built brands big enough to get sponsors and advertisers interested in their business or idea. You can score jobs based on your social media or brand power.

I was up for a movie a couple of years ago and I heard through the grapevine that it came down to another actress and me. It came down to who had more followers on social media. I got the role. Both of us were talented. Both of us would have performed well in the role. But I got the job based on the strength of my reach and brand. That's how important it is today.

One of the best opportunities for me to start my brand came a month after I had Kiyan. I got a call from Cris Abrego, whose production company owned this new reality space that included competition shows and fun versions of *Big Brother* on MTV and VH1, which were moving away from music and into this reality space.

Flavor of Love was getting astronomical ratings. And five to six million viewers were watching the reunion show. He asked me if I was available to host the reunion show for *Flavor of Love*. I said yes!

I had just had my baby, but I knew I couldn't stay out of the public eye for very long. Your brand is only as powerful as your level of success. Being out of the public eye for a long stretch would not help my brand. We're in a very "What Have You Done Lately" society. Out of sight, out of mind. People have short attention spans and even shorter memories. You have to keep your brand relevant.

So I was ready for the new challenge hosting a reunion show. What's great about being trained on live TV is that it prepares you to be ready for just about anything that can happen in television. There are no second takes on live

TV. And it made me the perfect host for these reality shows. No second takes. Most people are not trained on live TV. I always come in with something extra because of my experience. It has made me so much more valuable to people.

I hosted that *Flavor of Love* reunion show and every time 51 Minds had a reality show that had a reunion, they called me. I became known for hosting reality show reunions.

It was a lot of money for one job, but it was drastically different from knowing you're getting a check every week or every other week. Once a job wrapped, I'd say, "Oh, I'm unemployed again." But it kept me hungry and driven and constantly asking myself, "What's next?"

Part of building my brand was being the girl who could host those kinds of shows. The network folks said, "If she can control this crowd and keep it interesting in a reality reunion show, let's see what else she can do." I became valuable and there were producers and network executives and directors who were now seeking me out, the way Cris Abrego sought me out.

Everybody, it seems, has a reality show these days. And I get a lot of calls from people seeking advice for how to make it work for them. My advice to them: Use it as a tool to build your brand.

Doing reality television for me was a tool to build my brand and hence build my other businesses and help lead to other opportunities. I not only formed a production company, I also used the show to launch my makeup line and my clothing line, and to promote my books. Reality TV should be a thirty-minute commercial to promote whatever else you're doing. It shouldn't be your *only* life.

I learned this watching my friend Kim Kardashian, who is the queen of branding. She turned her show, *Keeping Up with the Kardashians*, into a means to promote and create other businesses—multi-multi-million-dollar businesses. I don't believe anyone understands the power of branding better than Kim.

She has more than twenty-five million followers on Twitter, and another twenty-three million on Instagram. When she announces something or says something on her social media pages, her fans (and even the haters) respond. When she posts a picture, she can break the Internet. Not many people can do that.

In 2014, Kim released a video game, Kim Kardashian: Hollywood, which made more than seven hundred fifty thousand dollars in just one day and was on track to earn more than two hundred million, according to published reports.

Branding!

I always drilled that into Dice and Po, two of my best friends, about appearing on our show.

"The show isn't going to be around forever," I'd tell them. "You'd better take advantage of this opportunity and use it to launch something that can sustain you for the long run. When I stop doing this show, you don't want to have five great seasons and not make it into anything else."

Po decided to start a recording career and got a record deal. Dice was still figuring it out when we stopped, but she decided to go behind the scenes. She's working with production companies now and she recently launched a clothing line, Roll the Dice, which features T-shirts and sweats in her style. It's pretty cool.

You have to figure out how to make whatever you're in work for whatever you want to do next. And if you aren't in a position to parlay your current gig into a business or another opportunity, then make sure it's helping to fund your dream or goal.

Make sure you work your day job and maximize your opportunities there, constantly looking for ways to get a better position or more money.

One of the best ways to move up the ranks in your current job is by becoming a poised and confident contributor to meetings and a presentation all-star. When you present information or ideas at work, it gives you an opportunity to publicly demonstrate your knowledge and, most important, show off your brand—that of a thoughtful, confident, capable woman.

As you begin to develop and boost your personal brand at work, you'll see presentations as opportunities to move forward. What you say or do in meetings, especially with high-level executives present, will influence the opinions of others. Just as I prepare for auditions by working with an acting coach and studying the script, you must seize the opportunity by preparing, practicing, and dressing the part.

Power players are never satisfied. They are always hatching plans to get to the next level. They are also very conscious about shaping and building their brand to get where they ultimately want to go.

If you're not Kim K. or me and if you don't have a reality show, you can still parlay your brand to build a career. I've seen people today who work a regular job, but also write a blog that they promote through social media and have built up quite a following. If you have a dream or a goal or a passion, use your brand to help you succeed in those arenas.

If you don't have aspirations beyond that, that's fine. If you are content working a nine-to-five or just having your career, make sure you don't do anything to ruin your brand. Make sure you're always in brand-protection mode because you don't want to jeopardize the position you're currently in.

Power players understand the power of their brand.

TIME-OUT

Place Boundaries on Social Media

Social media is there for a purpose. It's to make a connection. As we discussed in a previous chapter, what you post today on social media can have an impact on your future. It can cost you a job or an opportunity, so use that platform wisely.

I'm grateful that I didn't come up in the social media era. It has evolved. I learned to communicate before social media. So for me, it's a tool for branding and marketing, not just a way to talk to people.

You need to find the fine line between sharing and oversharing. How much of your life do you put on social media?

I tend to post very few personal pictures of my family and me—unless I'm sending a particular message. I hardly ever post anything with or about Melo. He has his own career and he has a right to have his privacy and share what he chooses. He wasn't on my reality show much. VH1 was constantly requesting more Melo, but I stood my ground.

I determined that my marriage is more important than a television show or ratings, and I wasn't willing to put that in jeopardy. I have seen so many people let social media and reality TV ruin their relationships.

There was a moment recently when Melo and Kiyan were taking a nap and they looked so cute together. I took a picture and I was about to post it. My friend Kelly Rowland (singer and member of Destiny's Child) was over and she stopped me before I hit SEND to Instagram. She told me to think about it.

"That's just for y'all," she said to me.

....

CHAPTER ELEVEN

The Crossover: Learn to Reinvent Yourself

*And as I reinvent myself and I'm constantly curi-
ous about everything, I can't wait to see what's
around the corner in newfound art and entertainment and exploration.*

—Pam Grier

Perception is reality, they say. So what do you do when the
perception of you doesn't line up with where you see yourself or where you want to go in your life or career?

You need a remix or to reinvent yourself. You will have
to put in the work to change perception.

When I first decided I wanted to become a serious
actress, I was up against a perception of me as "that girl
from MTV" or "that reality show girl." People in positions

of power to make decisions about hiring me for a role saw me only one way. So when I got roles they would be in line with how I was perceived.

To change the perception, I had to first change how people saw me.

I know a lot of people who let their past dictate their future options. Maybe you're not dealing with having an image of an MTV or reality TV show host while trying to break into serious acting roles. Maybe you're known as a party girl, and that's all people see. Now you want to embark on a career in corporate America and it's hard for people to see you in that role. Or maybe you want a promotion where you're currently working, but it's hard to shake the persona of an assistant, which you've been for a while. But people still see you as what you were, not what you're going to be. What do you do?

You change. Then you show those changes. You change people's perceptions of you by creating a new reality. Maybe you have to change how you dress, how you carry yourself, how you speak, even change the people you hang out with. Maybe you have to go back to school and get more training, a degree, or certificates. If it's important to you for people to see you differently, you have to first see yourself differently and then *present* yourself differently.

Maybe you were known as a slacker, someone without ambition, and people are reluctant to hire you or invite you to join them in opportunities because of your past. You will have to work to show them that you're no longer that person. That's *your* job to do. And you can't be mad at people for seeing you only the way they've always seen you.

Sinqua Walls, one of my castmates from *Power*, offered his place to me if I ever needed to shoot an audition. He has one of those places that's just perfect for it. My walls are full of art and if I need to do a scene with a plain background, I'd have to take art off the walls and move furniture.

I took him up on his offer one day and he shot my audition tape for me. When I was done he was so excited.

"La has been awakened," he said when he saw my tape. "You really know how to do this!"

My first thought was, "You work with me every day, don't you already know what I can do?" I guess in my limited role in the first season of *Power* perhaps he really didn't know I had range. He was surprised because while he worked with me, my small role at the time gave him only a limited view of what I could do. And we didn't shoot many scenes together. He must have had a perception of me that didn't fit with the role he saw me play in my audition. My work ethic, my attitude, and my professionalism were not in dispute. But he had to *see* me in the role before he could actually see me in the role.

I didn't take offense. I taped the scene. I took his reaction of me having been "awakened" after watching the taping as the highest compliment. I had proved myself to him. But I realize that I may have to keep proving myself to others. I may never just be given the benefit of the doubt. I can't be insulted. I have to just keep showing people who I am and what I can do.

People put people in boxes. You have to know what boxes people have you in in order to break out of them. I know when people see me they often see an MTV host or reality TV star, a so-called socialite, or the wife of Carmelo Anthony. I don't ignore those perceptions. I know what a huge stigma all of that is to overcome—especially the reality TV star one in light of how some of these reality shows depict women (or rather, women depict themselves). If some popular reality TV show star says, "I'm going to be a serious actor," it's only natural for people to think, "Yeah, right!"

But there have been quiet a few who have broken out of those boxes. Bethenny Frankel, from *The Real Housewives of New York,* was able to break out and have a stint as a nationally syndicated talk show host. And NeNe Leakes from *The Real Housewives of Atlanta* has not only appeared on scripted television shows like *Glee* and *The New Normal,* but also has starred on Broadway as the evil stepmother in *Cinderella.*

They have broken out of their boxes.

I knew that in order for me to realize my goal as a serious actor, I too would have to not just break out of my boxes, but also destroy them.

If you want to reinvent yourself, here's what you can do:

- See yourself the way you want to be perceived. What's your ultimate vision for who it is you want to be?

- Have a plan. You have to know how to reach that place. What steps must you take to become the person you want people to see? Will you need special training? What will you need to eliminate or add to your character to reach your goal?

- Reinforce that vision for yourself. Write down the things you want to change or become and leave notes for yourself in places where you are forced daily to see them. I believe in visual aids and even repeating phrases to yourself like, "I will master my craft."

- Surround yourself with people who honor your new self. You don't want people dragging you down or reminding you of or feeding that negative rendition of yourself. Avoid those people like the plague.

- Don't quit. You may not always live up to this new vision you have for yourself. But don't

quit. Consistency is the key. This will be a
life change. Be patient with yourself and don't
give up.

As I was reinventing myself, I was empowered because
I knew that I could. I could see it. It wasn't a task that was
so far out of reach. I had to work more with the perception
of others rather than making wholesale changes within
myself. My work came in the form of training, which I was
more than willing and able to do. With the confidence
that I had put in the work needed to deliver this new vision
of myself, the rest was just about showing people the
changes.

While it was all very doable, it wasn't easy. As I've said,
acting wasn't natural to me. But it didn't stop me from
working hard to get to the point where I was good. But I've
been doing that my whole life.

When I was sixteen and decided I wanted to work in
radio, I had to show that I was ready for the opportunity.
I couldn't present myself as an average teenager. I couldn't
come off as young and inexperienced. I had to present the
image of myself that I knew would land me the job.

They say, fake it until you make it. That is part of reinventing yourself. You may not be the person that you
want people to see . . . yet. But if you work on being that
person every day, the process alone will have people seeing
you differently.

There's a young man I know who wanted to rise in the ranks at the company in which he works. But his attire was very young and hip-hop. He had a beard that was unkempt and wild and the way he carried himself was very young. I asked him, "Is this how the bosses dress?"

He wanted to be a boss, but didn't understand that no one would see him as a boss the way he was currently carrying himself. He would need to start paying attention to what people in power were doing and emulating their ways.

I'm not saying that he should change who he is on the inside. But the outside perception matters. If you see yourself in a certain position or want to achieve a particular goal, look at those who are already there, and make sure you do the work to look like what it is you want people to see in you. If you want to be a CEO, starting looking, acting, and sounding like a CEO.

I wanted to be considered a serious actress, so I also made sure to take roles that showed my range. In the movie I'm working on as I'm writing this book, I'm playing the role of a thuggish lesbian. I have never played this kind of role before and I took it because it would show that I could do something that was completely different from the roles in which people were used to seeing me. It's a low-budget independent film. But it's important to have it among the kinds of things I can do.

While shooting this movie in Detroit, I learned that

one of my cast members, Rob Riley, is also a professional photographer. During one of our breaks, I asked him if he would take some shots of me in character on one of our days off. This was a big deal because a day off on an independent film is a rare occasion and people like to do their own thing. But he spent his day off doing this for me in the freezing cold and I really appreciated it. I posted those images on Instagram, but I also now use them in my portfolio so that people have a visual.

Telling someone what you can do isn't as effective as *showing* them. I can say, "I'm versatile and I can play any role." But when I show them through video clips or photos, they can actually see it for themselves.

I love watching people defy perceptions and break out of the box people put them in. It inspires me.

The biggest example of someone I know who reinvented himself is Mark Wahlberg. I first met him as Marky Mark while I was hosting on MTV. He was the front man of the hip-hop group Marky Mark and the Funky Bunch and they had a hit song, "Good Vibrations," which was number one on *Billboard*'s Hot 100 in 1991. He was known for being a bad boy and not wearing a shirt and being very buff.

Today Mark Wahlberg is one of the most sought-after actors and producers in Hollywood. He is a major power player. Everyone wants to work with him. I don't know all that he had to do to break out of that box he was in, but he did it. Hardly anyone remembers him as Marky Mark from the Funky Bunch.

Laz Alonso is another actor I really admire for his ability to reinvent himself. I'm sure many people don't know that Laz has a business degree and started his career on Wall Street as an investment banker at Merrill Lynch. His first break came as a host on BET, doing things similar to what I was doing at MTV. He was the BET version of a veejay and he also appeared in a couple of music videos.

He was able to break free from that image and became a serious actor. He has starred in *Stomp the Yard*, *Avatar*, and my favorite, *Miracle at St. Anna*. He has totally reinvented himself.

I have a friend named Gigi who was a stripper in a very popular strip club. She was known as one of the best strippers in the game and for her it wasn't just about gyrating naked on stage. Gigi saw her career as art, as a well-honed skill. Gigi's acrobatics and tricks on that pole would give the folks at Cirque du Soleil a run for their money.

A few years ago she decided she didn't want to strip anymore. She questioned how long she could keep stripping. Nobody is showing up to the club to see a fifty-year-old stripper, plus how long could she stay as flexible and keep her body in that kind of shape? So she was planning ahead and figuring out her next move.

She saved her money and opened a studio where she teaches pole dancing as a workout class. Pole-dancing classes have become a bit of a craze across the country, with women seeing the benefits of not just learning some of the risqué moves, but also the core training they get from doing it. It's a great workout. And Gigi has turned her past career into a successful business. She is doing extremely well.

Gigi figured out how to reinvent herself by taking what she already was good at and turning it into a business where she could teach others.

I'm always inspired when I see people like Gigi, Laz, Mark Wahlberg, and even Queen Latifah and LL Cool J—who have both parlayed their rap careers into television, film, producing, etc.—because they all figured out how to reinvent themselves and find tremendous success.

They may be celebrities or famous, but the process that they all went through is a blueprint for anyone. Again, it starts with first seeing yourself beyond where you are now, and taking the leap to actually roll up your sleeves and do the work. You can do it if you really want it.

It is so powerful to be able to change your life and change your future.

CHAPTER TWELVE

Salary Cap: Don't Chase Money, Chase Your Purpose

Money won't create success—the freedom to make it will.

—Nelson Mandela

I'm married to a man who has a lot of money. But when I think about my money, it's only *my* money that I'm counting. Melo's money is his money. He earned that. And while we're definitely in a partnership, psychologically it's important for me to never calculate his money as part of my wealth.

I've done well on my own accord and that makes our relationship even more solid because I'm not dependent on him to survive financially. I know he would do anything for me, and yes, we work as a team and yes, we are very much a unit, but when it comes to money I believe a person must build his or her own wealth. The process of working toward your individual goals—financial, career, etc.—is a major power play.

No matter how well off your mate or significant other is, I believe it is extremely important that you are self-sufficient, especially for women. When you depend on others for your very existence, you are literally handing over all of the power over your life.

You don't have to aspire to be rich, but at the very least you must be able to take care of yourself, no matter what.

One of the most important purchases I ever made was when I bought my first home in Los Angeles. It was a modest house—something I could afford at the time. But it was mine and no one could take it away from me. There was enough room for me and my family and my name was on the deed. That was an empowering moment in my life. I not only felt like a grown-up. I felt the freedom in that moment of ownership.

I believe that you need to work for everything you earn. I don't want to ever be complacent and feel as though I can just sit back and coast through life. It does something for your self-esteem, especially as a woman, to not depend on a man or your parents, or anyone, for that matter, to make a living or have a life.

My friends often joke, "La, you work like you're short on your rent!"

It is a running joke, but what many don't realize is that I work like this not for the rent or a check or the money. I work because work—acting and running businesses—is my passion. Work empowers me. Work fulfills me and makes me feel complete. I work because I have goals I want to achieve that I can only attain by working as hard as I do. I don't say, "I want to make this much money at the end of the year."

I don't have "things" goals. If there is a big-ticket item that I want, I will plan for it. And there are things that I can just buy because I can. But that's not how I measure my wealth or my success.

"What's enough money? How much do you need that will make you feel comfortable?" I've asked these questions in my group of friends and family and what's fascinating to me is how different that amount is from person to person.

Dice will say one number, Po will answer with another number. My brother will have an entirely different amount. And my "comfort number" will be something different altogether. Money is relative. Wealth is relative. You can ask ten people what amount will make them comfortable and you will get ten different answers. For someone, one hundred thousand dollars is his or her sweet number. They are working in a job that pays well and they love it and, for them, one hundred thousand dollars allows them to travel the way they want and have something saved for a rainy day. They have all of the material things they want and that amount will make them comfortable. For someone else, perhaps it's a million dollars.

"If I had a million dollars I would be set for life!" I've heard a friend say. "I could work that money and never have to work another day in my life."

For some, having a large lump sum like a million dollars means a certain kind of freedom. They may see an opportunity to invest that money and make it grow and give them the foundation to not have to work. Perhaps that's their goal—to never work again and live off the money that their money is making. That's their comfort.

Whatever the number, it's clear that it's never really about the money, but rather it's about the freedom or ability to do what you want because you have that money. It's about achieving the success you set out to achieve. It's about power. Personal power to control your own destiny, your own path, your own vision for your life.

I didn't realize how unimportant money was until I had it.

While I was growing up, a million dollars seemed like the craziest amount of money in the world. I couldn't imagine having a million dollars. For sure, I knew that if I ever had a million dollars I would be satisfied for life. I remember when that actually happened. Checking my bank account one day and seeing a million dollars in the bank—not in assets, retirement funds, real estate value, etc., but in my bank account—was a wild experience.

"Holy shit! I actually have a million dollars," I said to myself. I was really proud to have reached that milestone. It was money I had earned over the years doing the things that I loved. I was working toward other goals in radio and television on my way to becoming a millionaire. The moment of reaching a million wasn't nearly as important as what I was doing to get there.

That's when I knew for sure that you can't chase money; you have to chase your passions.

This work is not about reaching a monetary goal. It's always about the work, the opportunities, meeting new people, spending time with great people, and producing great works.

When I took the role in that small-budget independent film, I probably spent more money during the filming than I actually got paid. But I got to work with some incredible actors with whom I bonded and who taught me so much. Beyond what I learned professionally on this film, I now have some really special connections and friendships that I wouldn't have had had I not taken the film. Had I been all about the money, my life wouldn't be as enriched.

I know many people for whom it's all about the check. They won't take a job unless a certain dollar amount is being offered. "What are they paying me?!" is all they want to know.

I know people who are trying to break into certain fields, yet they are unwilling to intern or volunteer. They don't realize the power of making connections with people who can help them reach their goals or learn valuable skills or gain valuable information.

I wouldn't have nearly the experiences I've gained over the years or have the kinds of great people in my life today if my attitude was all about the check.

I take jobs because they fulfill me. I take jobs because they challenge me. I take jobs because they honor the goals I've set for myself as a person and professionally and they will help me get there. I take jobs because of the people involved. Money is somewhere at the bottom of the list of why I take a job.

When I was younger, money motivated me a whole lot more. Even then I had no perspective on it because I would have taken that job in Los Angeles for a whole lot less. But my main motivation then wasn't necessarily the money, either. It was the freedom and the power that money gave me. I never wanted to have to ask anybody for anything. I wanted to do it on my own. I didn't want to have to go to my mother and ask her for money when I knew how hard she was working.

I never wanted to ask my dad to pay my rent or help me buy a car. I wanted to be a grown-up and being a grown-up meant handling your business. In order to do that, you needed money. But I didn't crave a wild amount. I was content with being able to do things for myself and as long as I had enough money to do the things I wanted to do, I was happy.

Now that I'm older, the motivation is being able to bless others with my success. The pleasure in making money now is that I'm in a position to make sure my mother never has to work another day in her life.

All of the hours I put in are worth it because it makes it possible to be able to take care of her for everything she has done for me.

If anyone in my family needs anything, I can be there for them. That's what money does for me. It buys me the ability to take care of those around me, which is one of my purposes in life.

The problem with making money your focus is that you will never feel satisfied. It will never be enough. At some point, you'll realize that the money chase is unfulfilling. You'll always need more. You will look up one day with perhaps all of the money in the world and ask yourself, "Why did I do this?"

If you don't find your purpose in the midst of chasing that dollar, you will not be happy.

On the other side are the people who say, "I don't care about money!"

Well, if you don't care about money, you will probably never have it. Not ever having enough money is worse than having money and no purpose. Marriages fail over concerns about money. And people who don't have enough money to make ends meet don't have freedom and power to make choices in their lives. In fact, a lack of money will make some people make very bad choices out of desperation.

Money is important, but it can't be the end goal.

My mother asked me a while ago, "How does it feel to not have to worry about money?"

"Ma, it's something I actually never think about," I told her.

I'm sensitive to those around me who don't have it like that. I do know when I hear my friends complain about prices, I have to take a step back. I try to stay in touch by making sure I do my own shopping and stay aware of what's going on. I know what a gallon of milk costs because I've bought a gallon of milk recently.

I went to the movies with a group of friends and one of them said, "Damn, they're charging seventeen dollars for a popcorn and a soda?!" That's not a lot of money to me. But I do understand that it is for most people and I can't be in a bubble and not be aware of that.

I keep friends and family around me who ground me in that way. I never want to be so out of touch that I can't connect with my friends and family who are still working to make ends meet. Some of my best friends in the world are not celebrities and don't make a whole lot of money. When we hang out, I will often pick up the check because I can. Why would I expect someone I care about to even split the bill? I'm enjoying their company and if I invited, then I'm picking up the bill.

While this is the case, I also know that I can't always give a helping hand because everyone's journey has to be his or her own. Giving someone money or setting them up without them asking is also a formula for failure and resentment. Outside of your parents, doing this for friends and family can be a crutch that will render them powerless. You can offer a helping hand or an assist, but in doing so you have to make sure that you aren't getting in the way of someone's journey toward finding their power.

But I will definitely splurge on my friends. If I invite everyone to Vegas with me, best believe they will not have only their hotel and flight covered, but also money to gamble. Who wants to go somewhere and watch you spending money and having fun while they have nothing? I won't invite someone somewhere who can't afford it and not make sure that they are involved in all of the fun and activities.

Because I am blessed, I don't feel burdened by it. This is my family. These are my friends. That's what you do for the people you love. They're not asking for it or expecting it.

I'm not saying you do it with everyone. But when it's

your core group of friends, that's what you do. But I'm not paying their rent, buying them cars, and giving them money just because. There are lines. You have to find them and stay within them.

I made some mistakes around money when I was young.

One of the rules I live by today is to never borrow money, no matter what. Borrowing money can put you in a very awkward situation and if you can't pay it back, it can change the dynamics of your relationship. Even if you do pay back the debt, there will always be this unequal balance in the relationship. There is the possibility that the person who lent it could hold it over your head forever.

One of the few times I borrowed money, I actually had a pleasant experience. But I understood later how very wrong that could have gone.

Some people use money to gain power over others.

When I moved to Los Angeles I needed a car. It's a must-have living in Los Angeles, unlike New York or even Atlanta, where public transportation is just so easy to get to and convenient.

And while I was making more money than I ever imagined at the time, it would take a couple of months before I would be able to save up enough money to buy the car I wanted.

There was a very popular manager of artists who would be at the radio station all of the time with one artist or another who befriended me. He took me under his wing. His name was Fred Crawford and I called him Uncle Fred. I told him that I really wanted this Mercedes SUV. But I couldn't afford the down payment and I didn't want to settle for just any car. I was in Los Angeles, Hollywood, no less. I was young and wanted to fit in.

Uncle Fred offered to lend me the money for the car.

"I know you're good for it," he said. "Besides, I know where you work."

After taking the money, I realized I was in over my head. I hoped I would be able to pay him back because I really wasn't in a position to do so. I miscalculated how much take-home pay would be.

This was the first time I learned about budgeting and savings. I made sure I was very frugal—no dining out and partying. I tried to save every dime over the next few months.

It also helped to put things in perspective. You couldn't tell me that I didn't need a Benz. But as I was working to pay back this loan, I realized that it really wasn't important. I didn't need a Benz.

I did pay back the loan. But there was a valuable lesson in it for me. And while Uncle Fred never mentioned the loan, and never used it over me, I knew I was just lucky that he was a good person. He never had to ask for that money back, but it just felt like such a dark cloud over me. I felt funny around him as long as I owed him money. It wasn't coming from him; it was totally coming from me.

Money, in so many ways, is the root of a lot of evil. That's why I say don't borrow and unless it's really a special circumstance, I would say don't lend either.

If you lend someone money and they promise to pay you back by April and April comes and they can't pay you back, they start to act funny. If June, July, and August roll around and they still can't pay you back, I've seen the borrower get an attitude or have issues with the person who lent the money—even if that person never mentions it.

If that person simply can't pay you back at all, it is most likely that the friendship or relationship is ruined. And if they finally are able to pay you back, it's like a grudge. Or they pay you back in increments. You didn't lend it in increments, but you now have to get your money back in dribs and drabs. And if it is perceived that you don't need your money back, that becomes a thing, too.

If you wanted to give someone a gift, you would have given them a gift, right?

I try to avoid lending money at all costs.

If I do, it's after very careful thought. I assess who is asking, what their character and track records are. It's not about whether I need the money back but I have to assess our relationship and if it can withstand the loan. Because while I may not care if they can pay me back, I can't control how the borrower will feel.

I have to take each situation and assess it as it comes.

Melo's niece got a job working in New York City. She is doing amazingly well and is a great worker. Her boss has reached out to us to let us know how well she's actually doing. She's twenty years old and for her living in New York is a bit much. It is one of the most expensive cities in the world and while she has a great job, the pay isn't quite enough to live the way she should live.

If she asked to borrow money from me, I would give it to her. I'm seeing the work she's doing and she reminds me of myself at that age. I wouldn't hesitate to lend it, and I wouldn't even want that money back.

But she hasn't asked. And probably never will.

Then you have others who feel entitled to *your* money. They ask all of the time. They see you have it and feel like you should just lend them money. Period.

"You know you got it like that," they may say. "Pay my mortgage."

I get asked that all of the time. When people feel entitled or obligated, I'm more likely to stay away and avoid them. I don't like feeling that I have to do something. Because I don't.

The big thing to understand about money is that it is a tool; it is a means to an end. It's not the end.

If your passion is to start a business, make sure you

pursue that goal in your time away from your job. Don't leave that job until you know for sure your business is going to succeed.

Make sure you are totally prepared to pursue your passion before leaving your job—especially if you have children. Also, what you can do in your teens and twenties may not play the same in your thirties and forties. Not that you can't pursue your dreams in your later years. But the consequences are more dire if you don't succeed.

If there is something you really want to do, or want to have, save for it. Even if it takes you longer than expected. That time you take saving will also give you time to think about whether it's something you really want. If the answer is still yes after you've put considerable time into your savings, then you know it's real. You'll know that's truly your passion.

The more you follow your passions and your purpose, somehow the money will soon follow. Make that your focus, not the money.

CHAPTER THIRTEEN

The Power of Africa: Balance, Priorities, Freedom

You always learn a lot more when you lose than when you win.

—African proverb

I spent a couple of weeks in the summer of 2014 in South Africa. It was a life-changing experience—one that I didn't expect to have. I'd always wanted to go to Africa, but it was Kelly Rowland who convinced me to actually go. She and her husband, Tim, had traveled there a few months before and she called me as soon as she got back and told me if I didn't do anything else in life, I needed to take this trip.

I had a lot going on at the time—as usual. I had my day to day with Kiyan and Melo. There were auditions, tapings, parties, and red carpets to attend, but Kelly was insistent.

"This trip will change your life!" she told me.

I decided I would make it a family affair. I would invite my mother, my brother, his son Mekai, along with Melo and Kiyan, and we would all have this experience together.

It was a fifteen-hour plane ride and I was nervous and excited. We had actually just stopped our lives for a couple of weeks to do this.

When I stepped off the plane, everything was immediately different. Being a celebrity wasn't important there. Being a world-class athlete wasn't important. The blogs. The reviews. The entertainment news. The sports reporters. Not important.

We were living in the moment in Africa. We were going on a safari or to town. Nobody cared who we were. And it was refreshing. So refreshing to the point that I didn't care either. I usually can't get enough of what's happening in the entertainment world and will be on the Web sites all day talking about entertainment and fashion news. I didn't care about any of that.

Before we left, I had just finished wrapping *Think Like a Man Too*. I was in the midst of a whirlwind of activity around my career. I had just signed up to be in the new television series *Power*. Carmelo was in the middle of a major contract negotiation, and there was a lot of media speculation around whether or not he'd be staying with the New York Knicks. Our lives were on full blast. And here we were in Africa. Not important. We were out of the loop.

This would normally send me into an anxiety attack, not being front and center. I normally find myself worried that people will forget about me. I worry about keeping my brand up.

But none of that mattered here.

I met some very successful and powerful people there in Africa. I met a guy whose father is one of the wealthiest men in South Africa. But none of them were on Instagram or Twitter, worried about their brand or social media or the blogs. None of them were caught up in the nonsense.

I had been so busy, literally—traveling from Los Angeles to New York, then to Miami, auditioning, filming, chasing a dream, making sure I stayed on top—I didn't realize how exhausting it all was. Until I stopped completely. And breathed. What I learned hanging out with those real powerful people in Africa was that none of their success was based on superficial things.

I spent one of our evenings just talking with a few of our hosts about the world. We shared our perspectives and learned from one another. He didn't care who I was, or what he could get from me. He just enjoyed the conversation. *This* was powerful.

I left there thinking, "What am I doing with my life?

What am I going to leave behind? What is my legacy?" It can't be a bunch of pictures of me on the red carpet.

After I came back from South Africa, there was a little bit of sadness. I was left with a feeling that maybe I needed to reprioritize what is important. I started to really understand my dad and his perspective on life more.

My dad is a flight attendant and a free spirit. And he would always tell me about why he chose that career: "It has nothing to do with flying, or the job. Nothing. It's always about where I'm going."

For my dad, life was all about the experiences, having friends all over the world, and exchanging wisdom and knowledge. His job was a means to that end.

There are only a handful of places my dad has never been.

"It's about where I'm going and the people I'm meeting and what I'm experiencing," he'd tell me.

Coming back from Africa, I understood the power of that. I also understood that I needed more of that. I needed more balance in my life.

My upbringing was very balanced having a free spirit of a dad and a very stable, responsible, and serious mom. My mom was there for me through anything, and growing up, I needed that stability and support. I still do! But when I look at my dad, I get it now. If you look at pictures of my dad it looks like he's aging backward. And in every picture he has this big smile. He looks so happy.

Finding that place inside of you is true power. Living life by your own rules or as he says, "on the inside out," that's powerful. I understand why no matter what, he's always happy. He has found the meaning of life.

When I came back from the trip, my busy schedule was right there waiting for me. Instead of jumping right back into it, I took a minute to bask in what I had just experienced. I decided I would take some time each day just for me to reflect on what I'm doing. And I would take more breaks throughout the year—even if it's for a day or two—and not worry about what I was missing.

There has to be a balance in life. That's my inner turmoil. There's so much of my dad in me—the desire to get up and go, to see and experience the world, and not care. But there's way more of my mom, who will think first. I have responsibilities. But why does that mean I can't travel and do what I want to do? So I am finding balance.

I understand that I need to show my son that same balance. I'm the kind of parent who will take her son out of school for the year and take him with me to travel the world. He goes to a very good school when we're in New York, and when we're in Los Angeles he's homeschooled. But they could never teach him the things he learned in Africa on our vacation. He learns about sharing, socializing, and navigating personalities in addition to the three Rs in school. But life has so many valuable lessons that simply cannot be learned in school. I want my child to understand it's a big world and he needs to experience as much of it as possible.

I never want him to be complacent. I never want to be complacent. I never want to sit back and say, "This is my life." And that's it. I need to have a mix of the unpredictable with being responsible and doing the right things. I need balance.

My ten-day trip to Africa started in Johannesburg, South Africa. After we landed we drove for two and a half hours to The Shambala Game Reserve, where we stayed for four days.

Shambala is a retreat and almost indescribable. It is thirty thousand acres of peace, nature, and danger. It is home to lions, tigers, giraffes, and elephants, and they roam freely. They aren't tranquilized or sedated. This is their home. You are literally inside of their habitat.

On the drive to Shambala we passed through a few towns and I noticed that the air just smelled different. Kelly described it as somehow feeling closer to God. And it did. I don't know why, but being there you just felt more connected to that higher power.

We pulled up to the main gate and it opened into a world that I couldn't believe. Trees and grass and a vast plain as far as the eye could see. We were in a Jeep that was completely open. To our left there was a herd of zebras. To our right there was some sort of gnu or gazelle. Off in the distance we could see the giraffes eating from the tall trees. We could literally drive up to them and touch them. It was wild.

Whatever goes on in the jungle is what was going on inside Shambala. We were told not to feed the animals. They don't feed the animals. Nature takes its course out there. These aren't pets with names. Lions have eaten zebras. Predators and prey. Balance.

We were told we weren't necessarily in danger because the animals view the Jeeps as just big objects. They don't see the people inside as food. They don't attack the Jeeps. But they do come around the Jeep, which is very scary. Our guide told us that when that happens, just to be still and not to make any sudden movements. This wasn't some Siegfried and Roy or some other circus act. These animals weren't trained. And no one carries guns.

"We find that people act differently when they are armed," said our guide. "Trouble is more likely to happen when a gun is involved."

They operate on mutual respect. Our guides respect that we are in these animals' habitat, not the other way around. And we traveled in a way that tried not to intrude on their daily existence. It was humbling.

Melo and my brother went on a night safari. They said

the lions would acknowledge their presence but then paid them no attention. These were wild lions. But Melo said you had to respect the order of things and remain calm.

There were also black rhinos out there. They were usually in the distance. One time we stopped to look and were just parked and one seemed kind of far away. But he was getting closer and closer. And then I said, "Oh no! He's running toward our Jeep!"

Our driver angled the Jeep to cut him off. He met him at a slant so that he couldn't hit us head-on. He started battering the Jeep. And I was thinking, "Why the F aren't we driving away!"

Our guide explained that in the wild, you have to stand your ground against aggression. You cannot run or show fear. If you run, he will chase you and a black rhino is much faster than he looks. And far more dangerous. Once you stand your ground, the animal knows you mean business and he will go away. And he did.

I thought about that as it relates to power. A lot of times you will run into bullies, people who will try to run you over in business, at your job, or even in your personal life. But you have to stand your ground against them, not show fear.

My days in Africa were about letting nature take its course, experiencing it and learning from it. I was there with the animals, the dam, the lake and I saw the perfect order and balance of life. I didn't have to worry about a call time to be on set. No hair and makeup. No TMZ or Media TakeOut.

The guy who owns Shambala was close with Nelson Mandela. They built him a home on the grounds. We got to go on a tour of the house. It was wild to think I was in the room where one of the greatest men in history had walked, sat, read, and lived. I was in his bedroom and got to see the bed in which Mandela slept. There was a balcony off his bedroom where he would sit and watch the animals and read and write, I imagined.

I saw his books with his personal handwriting, notes and thoughts from Nelson Mandela. Powerful. He was a person who endured twenty-seven years of prison, hard labor, degradation. But he was fearless and powerful through it all.

Standing in his room, what most struck me was how bare it was. It was a beautiful room but it was minimal. There was a desk with a picture of Mandela behind the desk. There was a bed, a nightstand, and that was pretty much it. It wasn't cluttered or crowded. There was a lot of space to move around. It was, they said, just as he liked it.

As I sat at his desk in Shambala, I thought about him being locked away for so many years in a space no bigger than six square feet, and how this space with its openness and balcony overlooking this wildlife must have been freeing. I sat in the exact chair at his desk where Mandela sat, which was surreal if you think about it. I touched his books and I imagined him being in this room—open and free, the way he wasn't for so many years. This room was also free from things.

As I sat there all I could think about were the things we complain about and how meaningless and petty our complaints are. The things we work so hard for and how meaningless they too are, in the grand scheme of things. Mandela knew what was important. I had to take a moment and reflect on that. Reflect on Mandela's spirit, which was a study in balance, patience, courage, humility, and power.

From Shambala, we took a flight to Cape Town. Historic. We went to Robben Island, where Nelson Mandela spent eighteen of his twenty-seven years in jail. It was mind-blowing and sad, seeing where Mandela was locked up. The tour guide was a former prisoner of Robben Island, which I thought was so crazy.

"Why would you want to work somewhere that imprisoned you?" I asked.

He said it became his therapy to show people what happened there. I got a better understanding of what he and Mandela had to actually live through. It's totally different to read about something and actually experience it firsthand.

Imagine not having shoes. Being in a space about eight feet by seven feet. No electricity or running water. A bucket in the corner as your bathroom. That bucket staying in your cell with you until they decided to let you empty it. And that's your life for eighteen years. You work all day in a quarry breaking rocks. The sun beating on your head is so bright that it burns the retinas of your eyes. There's no shade, no relief. And that's your life. Your crime? Having the audacity to fight for freedom and equality for your people. Mandela endured this injustice with so much dignity. And his real power play when he was released—after all he had endured? Forgiveness.

When I think about complaining about anything, I think about Mandela.

When we got back from Africa, I went to see Kelly to thank her in person for encouraging us to go. I was so grateful to have a friend who, having experienced something so life changing, all she wanted to do was share it.

I know people who don't want anyone else to have whatever he or she has. People who don't want anyone else to experience happiness. You know people like that. It's as if they want to keep all of the good things for themselves and sharing it would somehow take it from them.

I'm blessed to have friends who are just the opposite. When Kelly traveled there with her now husband, she didn't even wait to get back to tell me. On the plane ride back to the States, she called us and said, "Our minds are completely blown."

While I learned about taking a moment, appreciating what you have and how to make sure your life is balanced,

I also learned the importance of having the right kinds of people in your life.

I would not have known about this without Kelly pushing me in that direction. I'm grateful to have people in my life who want me to grow and want me to experience new things. If your friends aren't like this, you need to reconsider if they are truly your friends.

Shortly after Kelly got back, she discovered she was pregnant, which she said made her reprioritize her life even more. She told me it was the trip to Africa that made her decision to put her career on the back burner for her marriage and new baby so much easier.

"The time is never going to be right [to have a baby]," she told me. "You have to just say, 'This is what I want to do now,' and commit to it and be happy. Because at the end of the day, what is really important?"

How do you prioritize what's important in your life? I would suggest you take a moment and write on a piece of paper the numbers one through five. What is the most important thing in your life? Write it down. What comes next? Write it down. Write down the top five most important things in your life. Then next to them write how much time you actually devote to those things.

If you say your family is number one but you spend more time on your career at number three, then either you're lying about your priorities or you're out of balance with your spirit. If your family comes first, let it show in your actions and deeds and your time. Of course, it's not always about time. But you can't say your significant other is really the most important person in your life when you neglect him or her and don't consider his or her needs.

I had to reprioritize when I came back. I put a whole lot of things in perspective and many of the things that had consumed my days no longer did. What I gained from Africa was a kind of freedom. The kind of freedom that Mandela had in that jail cell because no one can truly lock you up when your spirit is free. When you know who you are and why you're here and why you do what you do. When you know that, nothing else matters.

That's real power.

....

CHAPTER FOURTEEN

The Power of Elimination: People, Thoughts, Things

Some people are like dark clouds: when they disappear, it's a brighter day. Know when it's time to let go. Removing negative people from your life doesn't mean you hate them—it just means that you love yourself more.

—Anonymous

You can't be friends with someone who wants your life.

—Oprah Winfrey

Our social circles shape our worlds, and they can affect everything you feel, think, and do. Surrounding yourself with positive people and positive influences is key to achieving your goals in all areas of your life and living drama-free. For some of us, it's the people closest to us who create the most doubt in our minds, or bring the most negativity into our lives, or are the most jealous of our success.

It took me a minute to digest that quote from Oprah. But she's right. There is so much jealousy in the world. And there is no way to stop it. People are jealous sometimes and they don't even know it. Jealousy can seep into a friendship or relationship and ruin it. Once you spot it, you have to cut it off. It's the same way with negativity.

Family could be the worst people in your life. You look to them for approval, understanding, and support. But some family could be your worse enemies. I know how blessed I am to have a super-supportive family. But that's not the case with a lot of people. A friend of mine who is an entrepreneur told me that when he's working on a big idea he doesn't tell his family about it until it's already sold.

"I'd rather tell them when it's done because they will find a million ways to talk me out of it, or tell me why it's a bad idea and I shouldn't be doing it," he told me.

They may mean well, but negativity is negativity. If your family and those closest to you are being negative and unsupportive, you will have to cut them off—at least until you get so strong that their words and actions won't have any impact on your personal outcome. Or like my friend, keep things to yourself until you've accomplished what you've set out to do.

Friends can also be some of your biggest obstacles to success.

If you can look at someone else's life and ask, "Why them?" then you really have no understanding of your own path to success. You can't have people in your life that will ask that question of themselves because their life's focus is not on their path, but yours.

Each of us has our own power path. Why him or her? Because it was their path. Why not you? Well, you obviously are spending so much time thinking about and worrying about others that you haven't discovered yours. If you live your life looking at someone else's life wishing it were yours, you will never discover the purpose and plan for your own life.

It's easy to look at the success of others and see how great it is. But you don't see the obstacles, the failures, and the rough patches along the way. It looks so easy that everyone thinks they can do it. In defense of those who think that way, I understand this reaction. You may be just as talented and gifted, perhaps more talented than that person who is so successful. So it's natural to ask why not you.

My advice: Be content with you and your life. Embrace where you are and what you're doing. And strive to find your own place. If you focus on what you're doing and on being content with where you are in your life, there is no room for jealousy.

If you have people in your life who are jealous of you, you have to eliminate them. You can't have people who envy you, what you do, and what you have. They're like poison. Eventually, their energy will seep into your life and erode your progress.

Perhaps it's not a jealous person you're dealing with. Maybe it's just someone who is negative and always complaining. They, too, have to go!

As a friend or loved one you should be there as a shoulder to cry on, to provide advice and comfort. However, if there's a person in your life who offers nothing but negativity and complaints, they have to be eliminated from your life. They will drain you of your power and they don't bring anything to fill you back up. They have to go.

I used to want everyone to like me. I would do just about anything to get people to like me. As I've gotten older, I realize the importance of having people in my life who support me, who are positive and who empower me. I've also realized the power in pruning, letting go of dead weight, not having people around just to have them around.

Take stock of the people around you and detox your life by clearing out fake friends, and the players posing as life partners.

When I first started dating Melo, I had a friend who would always call me to tell me where he was and what he was doing.

"I hear there's a party in the city he's playing in later tonight," she would report. Or: "I heard that he was seen at such and such club. . . ."

Every conversation was about Melo and what he might be up to. I knew if my relationship with Melo was going to have a chance, she had to go. She was toxic and making me paranoid and either I would be questioning him about everything she said or I'd be driving myself crazy worrying about what he was up to when he was on the road.

She used to call me every day. But I started not answering the phone. Instead of talking to her every day, I would maybe answer the phone twice a week. When I did talk to her and she'd start with her Melo report, I would quickly change the subject. She never got the message and eventually, I weeded her out of my life.

She was a wonderful person, but I couldn't remain friends with her.

"Detox your life. Today is a new day, new beginning. Start now." That was my Instagram post on December 1, 2014. I had thousands of comments, mostly from people thanking me, telling me how I validated them, and how right I was. We all know it, but sometimes we need to hear it from someone else.

They say people come into your life for a reason, a season, or a lifetime. Power players know the difference and they don't try to keep a seasonal person around for a lifetime.

Just because a person is seasonal doesn't mean that their existence in your life wasn't meaningful. It just means that they served their purpose in your life or you served your purpose in theirs and in order for you both to grow, you have to move on.

To be honest, I have a hard time pruning people from my life. I don't think I've ever cut a family member. And with friends, it's also been difficult. I won't make a production out of it. I just avoid people. I don't like conflict and arguments. But when it's time to go, it's time to go.

In business, I also have a hard time. I've had managers, lawyers, and staff that I held on to much longer than I needed to because I didn't want to hurt anyone's feelings. I would avoid doing what needed to be done. But as I grow as a businesswoman, one of the most important things to learn is when to let go—when to move on. I hurt my business and delayed my progress and success by keeping people around who weren't bringing things to the table to help me get to the next level.

If you're working at your job and you want a promotion but all of your coworkers are content where they are or you hang only with the people whose pay grade is below yours, you should reevaluate that. I'm not saying you should cut them off, but how much time you spend with them matters. Birds of a feather flock together, they say. If you hang around people who have no ambition, it's not uncommon that they will be a negative influence on you.

You can be the strongest person in the world; it's just really hard to break free from certain energies. So watch your work friends/associates.

Letting go of people is a major power play. And while it may be hard initially, in the long run it will strengthen you.

In addition to people, letting go of negative and unproductive thoughts is probably the most powerful thing you can do. In acting class, one of our exercises involves writing on a piece of paper "bad actor" thoughts and replacing them with "good actor" thoughts.

For example:

I wish my _____ was _____
I'm not as _____ as _____
Life is so hard for me because _____

My bad actor thoughts included:

I'm not as good as Rosario Dawson. I'll never be as successful as she is.

I had to replace that bad thought with why I am good enough and what I bring to the table. I had to focus on my attributes, not someone else's in comparison to mine. It was a very valuable exercise. You never know how many bad actor thoughts you have roaming around your mind until you're forced to write them down.

You may think you're just not good enough, but in reality, your thoughts aren't good enough. Your toxic or bad actor thoughts can take you right out of the game.

I would sit in auditions, and I'd be in a room with so many other people auditioning for the exact same roles—familiar faces, famous faces. I would see people more seasoned than I am and start to think, "Of course, *she's* probably going to get the role! She just had a number one movie. They will never pick me over her."

I would count myself out, never thinking that maybe they wanted a fresh face for this one, maybe they were looking for something different. Or maybe I was exactly perfect for the role. I had already let my bad actor take over. I can't tell you how many times I messed it up for myself until I finally got it together.

Today, I don't care who is auditioning. All I'm thinking is that I'm going to go in there and I'm going to kill it. I'm going to give my all and own the role.

I have learned that thoughts are powerful.

I can think, "Yes, she's great, but I bring something different to the table." Or I can not even think about her and focus on what I'm going to do well.

I totally understand why so many of us count ourselves out. It's a defense mechanism so that we can give ourselves a free pass just in case we don't get the role, the job, the opportunity. But you're really setting yourself up for failure.

In my business, there are so few roles—especially for African-Americans and Latinas. You will usually see the same people at every single audition. More often than not, if it's a great role there will be so many people showing up who are more experienced or more accomplished than I am. But that doesn't mean that they are better than I am. And it certainly doesn't mean that I won't get the role. If I felt that way, I would just leave or not show up. But this is the career I want to have.

So I must eliminate the bad thoughts and make sure I'm feeding my spirit only the good food. Addition by subtraction is a power play.

Finally, declutter your life. Get rid of the excess baggage—emotions and thoughts that aren't helping you. Get rid of the excess people—folks that you just have around because they've always been there. Get rid of the excess things—papers and files that are cluttering your work space. Clutter weighs you down and prevents you from fully moving to your next destination.

In the last chapter I talked about Nelson Mandela and how the home he lived in during his later years was so free from clutter. I know so many people who complain about not being able to get things done, but when you see their desk, you're not surprised. How can you work successfully in chaos? You can't.

Take stock of the unnecessary things you are hanging on to. And get rid of them. There is something liberating about throwing things away. I have a friend who has a bonfire for her bills once a year. If she's paid them off, she takes all of the past bills and puts them in her backyard fire pit. You don't have to go to those extremes. You can shred paperwork you don't need. But the message for your future success must be: Less is more!

I do a clean sweep at least four times a year—once for each season. I get rid of numbers, papers, or even clothes I don't need. Having a messy desk or work area or even home represents you as someone who may not be ready for the next level.

The process of elimination can be a huge addition to your life.

CHAPTER FIFTEEN

The Assist: Be a Mentor

*It is literally true that you can succeed best and
quickest by helping others to succeed.*

—Napoleon Hill, author of
Think and Grow Rich

I would not be where I am today without the help of others.
Chaka Zulu gave me the biggest assist of my career early on.
When I was his intern at WHTA, he taught me everything
I needed to know about the radio business. I was ready
when I finally got my shot because of an assist from Chaka.

In acting, powerhouse producer Will Packer has been a
valuable friend, sounding board, and advice giver. Acting is
such a competitive field that you need someone to help you
navigate that space, or just be there to support you with a
word of encouragement. Will Packer has been that for me.

In business, my biggest mentor, champion, and help-mate has been Loren Ridinger, who runs Market America, where my makeup line was launched. She has not just been a super role model, but also helped me create my blueprint for success in business. I didn't know much at all about business until I met Loren.

Cris Abrego helped me launch my own production company and learn that business from the inside out.

It is virtually impossible to be successful in any career without help.

The saying goes, "Success has many fathers, but failure is an orphan," and it couldn't be truer. People will definitely come out of the woodwork to take credit for your success. But the reality is you would probably not be successful without a whole lot of helping hands. You cannot negate the kind word, the good advice, or the actual hand-holding that goes into your success. It could be a shoulder to cry on or a bed to sleep in that can make your experience go more smoothly.

When I moved back to New York from Los Angeles after getting the job at MTV, I had no place to stay. La-Ronda Sutton, who now works with Atlanta Mayor Kasim Reed, gave me a room in her apartment until I could find my own place. She didn't charge me rent or ask for any-thing. Not many people do that. I was so grateful.

When I found my own place in Edgewater, New Jersey, it was pretty pricey. I was making great money at

MTV, but the down payment of first and last month's rent as security was way beyond what I could save up in the couple of months I had been back in New York.

I just mentioned it to my good friend Trina and she just gave me the down payment for my apartment. Trina, who is one of dopest female MCs ever, whom I've known since I was a teenager on the radio in Atlanta, was doing really well and it was nothing for her. But it was everything to me. I will never forget her generosity. And again, she never expected anything in return. But the assist by LaRonda and Trina relieved the stress from my life during that time. I could focus on my new job and not worry about where I would live or how I would live.

You know the type of person you are by the type of people around you. And thinking back over all of the wonderful people who have come to my aid in my life, I consider myself pretty blessed.

I've been given a helping hand so much in my life that I know how important it is that I believe one of the major power plays is paying it forward, giving an assist where you can.

Giving an assist is not about giving things to people. It's literally being a bridge until they can do it for themselves. Or better yet, teaching them how to do it for themselves.

There is a saying: "Give a man a fish and he eats for a day, but teach a man to fish and he eats for the rest of his life." That, too, could not be truer. When I think about helping people, I always want to teach someone to fish because then you get to see them not just do for themselves but eventually be in a position to do for others, too.

In the spring of 2003, my brother Christian was running with a tough crowd. He had decided he wanted to be in the music business. He was going to be a rapper and while he wasn't raised in poverty or wasn't of the streets, he wanted that street credibility.

His journey took a left turn. One evening he was at a local gas station and a group of guys got into an altercation and they started shooting. He was at the wrong place at the wrong time and he was doing wrong things. My brother got caught in the cross fire, and he was shot in the stomach.

I was in New York and had just gotten off the air at MTV when my mother called me in a panic. I had never heard her so upset and when she told me what happened, my heart dropped. I got on the next flight and was there to see him through his recovery, which ended up being quite a journey.

We brought him home from the hospital after weeks in recovery. He had a colostomy bag, and he ended up getting an infection. It was very serious. The infection was almost worse than the actual shooting.

In addition to the physical stress and the emotions of seeing my brother struggle to get back to good health, we also had to deal with the police. There was, of course, an investigation and the way they treated my family was horrific. A young black man gets shot and there's a typical response by law enforcement. He was treated as if he was the criminal. And my mother had to deal with that while he was clinging to life. The police were very dismissive of my mom, who wanted answers, and they were also rude the way they talked down to her. It was so crazy how it all happened.

The road to recovery for Christian was a big deal, beyond the physical. Getting shot seemed to take him off his life path. He lost his zest for life. He was always a great person, but he was just down after this and not motivated to do anything. I get emotional just thinking about that period in his life.

But when I see him today, I understand the power of not giving up on someone. I have witnessed what happens when you empower someone.

A lot of times people want to help the people in their lives—whether it's their mom, their children, or even close friends—by giving them things. When you're successful, the temptation is just to lend a helping hand through a checkbook.

As the oldest child of my mother and father, I never felt any pressure to set the tone or be an example, but I have always felt a responsibility for Christian, who is four years younger. During this period in his life I felt helpless because I really didn't know what to do. But a few years later, I was able to provide an assist that changed his life.

I can talk to him about anything and he knows me better than just about anyone in the world. He will put me in my place when I need it. He's a chameleon, able to fit in with any crowd and work well in all environments. He has the gift of gab and he's charming. Girls like him and guys think he's cool. He's like me in that sense. He recently spent a couple of days with me on a movie set in Detroit and by the end of day one, he's hanging out with the entire crew at the club as if he was part of the movie.

With all of his natural gifts, he had a hard time finding his way. He went to college and after one semester discovered that school wasn't for him. Just being in ATL with the kinds of artists seemingly making it all around him, he felt that he could just jump into the rap game. But that wasn't happening. All he ended up with was hanging with the wrong crowd with no direction.

He had just had a child, then the shooting, and the message was clear that it was time to grow up and get it together. His recovery was slow and he was pretty down most of the time. It wasn't something that you could just talk him through. I wanted so desperately to help my brother get back on his feet, get back in the game. Instead of just "hooking him up" with things, I hooked him up with an opportunity.

A few years ago I was approached by Market America to create a makeup and beauty line, Motives for La La, geared toward women of color. It was something I had been thinking about doing for quite some time. While I don't wear a lot of makeup in my day-to-day life, I do love having something real simple to throw on when I have to head out. This line is exactly that. It's great for putting on just a little something—a light eye and a light lip—to head to the store. And it's definitely got all of the colors and shades for that evening out. But I loved the name— Motives—and the philosophy of motivating women to be their best selves. That was something I wanted to be a part of.

The other cool thing about Motives is that it can be spun into a business for women. Women can become salespeople and create their own business. It was a springboard.

As we were kicking it off, we needed someone to go around the country and let people know about this wonderful product line and the opportunities associated with it. The company needed someone who could get out there and get women excited about not just purchasing it, but also getting on board and starting their own business opportunity selling Motives for La La.

I knew this would be a perfect position for my brother.

With Motives, Christian found his passion. He is the type of person who loves being around people. He can blend with folks in the corporate arena as well as people on the streets. He loves women. What man wouldn't want to spend their days traveling around the country helping women? I knew it was something he would be good at.

And he was. Working for Motives for La La gave my brother a new lease on life. He wasn't working for me, per se, but he was working for himself. The way the company is set up is to create entrepreneurs and reward those who go that extra mile.

Within just a few months, my brother had made enough money to buy his own car. He bought a silver Jeep Wrangler, something he'd always wanted, and he bought it with his own money. The feeling of working hard and going to get something you've always wanted with your own money is incredible. I could have bought my brother any car he wanted, but buying his own car made a difference in his life.

He is a great father to his children. His girlfriend had two children and he's taking them on as his own. It's ironic because it's the exact same situation that he and I grew up in with our stepfather. I never knew how special my stepfather really was until I watched my brother with his children (we don't make the distinction between the stepchildren and his own). It takes a great man to raise someone else's children because you have to walk a very thin line. Looking back, I know how difficult that was for my stepdad and I have even more respect for him watching my brother do it.

Finding his own space was the incentive that led Christian to take his responsibilities to another level in every area—in his home and in his business. He's now a regional director for my Motives line and they are using him in other areas of the company, Market America. He recently bought his own home. He is rejuvenated. He is more active in life, and he smiles a whole lot these days—something he hadn't done for far too many years.

Even before my brother's health crisis, he wasn't really on a path to success. He was just kind of sleepwalking through life.

Sometimes life can throw you a curveball that could take you into the depths of despair, but if you ride it out, and seize the opportunities that come your way, you can turn things around.

On the other side of that, I believe it is the responsibility of those who are blessed with success to give an assist, to lend a hand. Not a handout. But in a hand up. Provide an opportunity for someone, an encouraging word of advice, pay it forward. Teach him to fish.

Being able to help people is perhaps the greatest reward of success.

My mom has always been there for us. She has been our steady rock. And it is my greatest pleasure to make sure she has everything she needs and wants.

She doesn't really get emotional and gooey. But she recently called me and said, "I just wanted to tell you thank you for making my life easier. The fact that I don't have to get up and go to a job every day, you made that happen. And I don't take it for granted. I love you. I just had an aha moment and I wanted to share with you that you are a wonderful daughter!"

I couldn't hold back the tears. Because all of the work I've been doing all of my life has not just been about building a career, but about my purpose—taking care of people. To be able to do that, give my brother an opportunity to get his life back on track, see that Mother never has to work another day in her life if she doesn't want to, keeps me on my grind.

The power in my success is that I'm able to do these things. When I'm exhausted and when I'm going through something and have to put on a face, I just remember what it's all about.

You have to be on steady footing before you reach that hand out to help someone, though. Helping people when you yourself aren't stable can pull you down. You have to be real with yourself. Are you in a position to actually help? If the answer is no, then when people ask you, you must have the power to say no.

The good news is that while you may not be able to assist someone in the moment the way they like, there are a host of things you can develop within yourself to be helpful to people. As I mentioned, some of the greatest assists I give to people are in the form of advice—which is free. But you need to be careful with that as well. Time is valuable and if you spend yours giving it to people and not taking care of the things you have on your own plate, you can be dragged down.

Remember Rule Number One: Love yourself first. If you're set and everything is right in your life, then you must look up and see where you can give back and help others. But you can't really be a mentor to someone else while you're trying to get it together yourself. I couldn't do any of these things for the people in my life while I was hustling to get to a place. But today I can.

It makes me happy to see everyone around me successful and happy. Success is rewarding only if you can help others achieve it, too.

Below are six characteristics of a mentor.

Become a Power Mentor

Mentoring other people has some great payoffs: You give back to others. You learn new things from your protégé. And it feels great. But being a great mentor doesn't mean simply giving orders and telling the person you're mentoring what to do. It's actually a combination of listening, offering advice, and letting the person you're mentoring figure out the best course of action on his or her own—including making some mistakes along the way.

Follow these six steps to become a power mentor:

1. Share your own experiences—especially mistakes.
When relevant, use your own life to illustrate the advice you give. Stories about your own successes and failures show how you make decisions as well as the real-world results and consequences of playing it safe or taking risks. Coming clean about the mistakes you've made makes you more human. Your protégé can see that success doesn't have to mean perfection.

2. Set the ground rules. Make sure you're both clear about what you expect out of the mentoring relationship, including how and how often you'll communicate and what you expect of each other. Talking through these expectations up front lessens the potential for miscommunication. It's also helpful to have a "trial period" when you test each other out and make sure the relationship is a good fit. Try working together for three or six months, then decide whether to continue.

3. Explore options. As you help your protégé navigate certain situations or shoot for specific goals, encourage him or her to explore new approaches and different ways of thinking. Being able to see situations from different viewpoints is an important quality in leaders.

4. Make introductions. You shouldn't be expected to hand over your phone's contact list, but you're probably more well connected than your protégé. A few strategic intros can fast-forward a project, job hunt, or new business opportunity.

5. Encourage giving back. Even those who are new to a profession can give back in some way. Encourage the people you mentor to act as mentors to others, perhaps helping students or other new professionals.

6. Know when to let go. At some point, most mentoring relationships have fulfilled their purpose, and it's time for both people to move on. When the time comes, let go gracefully. The best mentoring relationships transition into strong professional or even personal friendships.

TIME-OUT

Be a Power Source

Have you ever been around someone who makes you feel good about yourself—those folks who really hear what you're saying and give you spot-on advice and encouragement? I call them "power sources." They recharge us and give us glimpses of how truly amazing we really are, lifting our spirits and empowering us to go farther and be better. It doesn't take special training to be a power source, and you don't have to be born that way. Here are the six secrets of being a power source, so you can be one, too.

1. Listen. Power sources are good at hearing what the person is really saying. They don't always immediately try to fix the situation. Sometimes, people just want to be heard and have their feelings validated. Power sources know when to dive in with solutions and when to say, "I hear you, and it's no wonder you feel that way."

2. Emphasize others' strengths. Petty people feel better by tearing down others. Truly powerful people get more power by building up the people around them. When a friend, family member, or colleague comes to you for advice, re-

mind them of their strengths. Compliment them. When they do something amazing, say so. When people come to you for help or in distress, be a calming force, helping them find solutions using the attributes that make them unique and remarkable.

3. Deal with situations honestly. You don't do anyone any favors by lying to preserve feelings or encouraging bad decisions. Of course, you can't stop people from doing what they're going to do, but you can gently and kindly point out other options or the potential downside of moving forward with a bad plan or being fueled by negative emotions.

4. Help them see the positive. There's always more than one way to look at a situation. One person's disaster can be another person's new start. You empower people when you help them get out of the darkness and start seeing the light.

5. Avoid gossip. Power sources don't gossip or talk about others behind their backs. They operate in good faith and don't get caught passing along hurtful rumors or untruths.

6. Encourage action. Taking positive action is the best antidote to negative situations and attitudes. When everything seems bleak, help the people around you find and take one

small step that can change their situations. It can be anything from rewriting your résumé to getting out for a walk in order to think more clearly. Help the people around you find small, positive action. It's the first step to turning things around.

CHAPTER SIXTEEN

My Starting Five: Lessons Learned from These Power Players

Teamwork divides the task and multiplies the success.

—Unknown

Alone we can do so little; together we can do so much.

—Helen Keller

Every team needs a starting five. You cannot have a victory unless everyone plays their part on a team and they work together. In basketball, there are always debates about who's the best at each position. Michael Jordan, Larry Bird, and Magic Johnson are usually on everyone's starting five. They are selected because of their winning qualities, more so than their athletic abilities. They are the quintessential team players who make everyone around them better.

In life, we also need a team. Elders, mentors—people who have given you a road map for success, either by example or direct contact. They have the qualities that it takes to win in life. You can follow their example and not have to make so many mistakes on your own (although mistakes sometimes are the building blocks to success).

There are people who I admire dearly and whose stories and experiences have taught me many valuable lessons.

This is my starting five:

1. At point guard is my grandmother, Mami Nina. She was the matriarch of my family and a woman who I not only admire but also hope to emulate. My grandmother was fearless.

As a young woman living in Puerto Rico, she was the star of her town. She was the first one to go to college and was very successful. If you go back to her town, people remember her. She had that kind of impact.

She married my grandfather and their marriage was rocky at first. They had a falling-out and she decided to leave. This was during a time when women didn't leave;

they stuck it out no matter what. My Mami Nina wasn't having it. She didn't just leave my grandfather; she left the country—leaving everything familiar and comfortable—and went to New York, where she had nothing. It was a lot like me getting on that plane to Los Angeles. Part of the courage of doing that was because of my grandmother.

She must have been scared. She took her two children and left. She was prepared to be a single mother in New York City with no job prospects. She had nothing but her boldness and belief in herself. And she made it. I think it's so powerful to leave the man you love because you're not happy. Then to leave the life you have in a town in which you're revered, to go to a place where no one knows you and you know nothing.

She arrived in New York and moved into the Marcy Projects—a far cry from her beautiful Puerto Rican neighborhood. But in the Marcy Projects my grandmother found her power. My grandfather eventually moved to New York to be with her. He worked to patch things up. That's powerful to me, too. My grandmother didn't go back. She didn't change her mind when it was tough and turn back. My grandfather came to her. He followed her. She forced a change in him.

Power.

My mom was the first one of her children born in New York. Mami Nina and my grandfather had three more children after my mom, so I guess they got it together. But it took my grandmother's power play to make him step up and bring the family back together.

Power says you're prepared to do it alone if you have to. Power doesn't depend on having someone else to rescue you. That's why my Mami Nina leads my team.

2. Coming in at the other guard spot is my mom. She and my grandmother have always looked over me, prayed for me, protected me, and they have both given me the best examples for me to become a successful powerful woman in my own right.

My mom is a power player. Looking at her life and the sacrifices she made, I see she unleashed her power in a much more subtle way. Her power is quieter. And it shows up in places that most wouldn't see it.

It was my mother who allowed me at sixteen to spread my wings and follow my dreams. Even if she was scared for me, she never let me know. She let me use her car and she was supportive, even if to the world it may have looked crazy as hell. She put the needs of her children before her own. When things weren't going well for me in New Jersey, she too left everything behind and moved us to Atlanta. I know her life might have been more secure in New Jersey with my stepfather, especially financially. But my mother always put us first.

Letting go of something you love so much is perhaps the hardest thing to do, but my mother did that for me.

She didn't nag me about dropping out of college, and she didn't push me into going back or going to a trade school. She trusted that I would find my way because she also knew she had instilled some pretty awesome values in me. I really don't know what it's like not to be supported because I've been supported my entire life.

I know my mom had some hard times. I know for a fact she did. But she never brought any of that pain into our home. I don't ever recall seeing her cry when we were growing up. And I think I've only seen her cry twice in my entire life. She would always have a brave face no matter what she was going through.

Now that I'm a mom, I understand why. It's so important that your children feel safe and secure. And when Mom is broken up, children get scared and anxious. I could definitely tap into my mom's strength with that one. I try my best to have a brave face with Kiyan at all times. And I take my moments when I'm alone. This is probably what my mom did. She worked admissions at a hospital and had to be there at eight every morning. She was never late. I'm sure she had horrible days at work. But we never knew it.

I appreciate my mom. And I understand life so much better for having her as a mother.

3. At the power forward spot is Oprah Winfrey. I met her once when the USA Basketball Team won the gold medal. She invited all of the players onto her show. She was gra-

cious and wonderful. I became very close to Gayle King and I will always tell her, "Tell Ms. O I said hello." And she does. So I can say that Oprah Winfrey knows me, which is really cool.

But what puts her on my starting five is the standard she has created for how to conduct yourself in the media and business. As I grow as a businesswoman, I channel Oprah Winfrey. She has so much grace and power that I would love to be able to just emulate that spirit.

The other reason why she's so powerful to me is that her career arc is one I'd like to follow. She started out in radio as a newscaster. Then she was on television, reading the news. She was able to parlay that into a talk show. From there, she started acting.

I'm so into people who can prove to the world that they can do many different things. As you know, I hate being put in a box. And Oprah Winfrey is the ultimate box cutter. Radio, television, her own show, acting, producer, the owner of a magazine and a network. Those are footsteps I would love to follow.

My career has changed so many times. I put on so many hats. Watching Oprah handle it all gives me inspiration that I can, too. And the acting? Oprah in *The Color Purple, The Butler,* and *Selma,* it doesn't get much better than that. It's not like she's getting these jobs because she's Oprah Winfrey. She's earning these roles and she's killing it! I can't see anyone else playing Miss Sofia in *The Color Purple*. Can you?

4. At the other forward spot is the First Lady of the United States of America, Michelle Obama. I've had the pleasure of being around her on several occasions. She and the president are huge basketball fans and they love Melo. They even know Kiyan. To just be able to say that I know the first lady and the president is pretty awesome.

But what makes Michelle Obama part of my starting five is her ability to be a regular person. I don't know anyone personally who handles so much responsibility and power with such grace. She is not just warm, but also down to earth. It feels as if she's just one of the girls kicking it. But she's the first lady!

I know some celebrities who could take a few lessons in humility and humanity from her. Michelle Obama is someone you can talk to and share your thoughts and dreams and problems with and she listens and gives advice. She makes you feel as if she is your friend.

I can't imagine her life with the Secret Service and the inability to do regular things. The celebrity life is only a hint of what kind of lockdown she's in every day. But she doesn't wear any of that.

The most powerful people are often the ones who you don't see coming. But all you need to do is check Mrs.

Obama's background. She was raised on the South Side of Chicago. Her mom was a secretary and her dad worked at a city water plant. She excelled in school, graduating with honors from Princeton University, and then with a law degree from Harvard. She met President Obama at Sidley Austin, the law firm where they both worked. She was assigned to be his mentor when he arrived as a summer associate.

While she has that powerful background, what I love most about Michelle Obama is that she knows how to play her position. She doesn't have to flex and show that she's smart and brilliant and powerful. She is. She is powerful enough to be first lady and stand beside our president and support him.

Michelle Obama is fit, she's smart, she's stylish, she's hip. A powerful role model for all women.

5. My center is literally the center of my life and perhaps the most powerful person on my team—my husband, Carmelo Anthony. I love him immensely. But what I love most about him is how much he's willing to grow and challenge himself.

I'm with him on a day-to-day basis and while some people think they know him because they cover him for a newspaper or magazine or television outlet, I actually see the time and effort he puts into working on himself and his craft. His work ethic is unlike anything I've seen. It's crazy to see the kind of dedication he puts into his career.

But just as much as he works on his fitness, and his teamwork, he brings all of that home, too. He is just as dedicated as a husband and a father. When I see him with Kiyan my heart melts. When I mentioned my mom always putting on a brave face for us, that's Melo.

He could be having the worst day ever, but when he walks through that door, he is smiles and warmth with us. He may share some of his frustrations with me one-on-one, but with Kiyan, it's all love and talking about how his day was at school and what he wants to do for the night.

I don't know how he does it because some of these days can be pretty brutal, especially if he had an off night or his team is suffering through a losing streak. Even I have a hard time keeping it together.

I have been with Melo so long and I must say that he just keeps getting better with time. I have watched him evolve and mature and grow. And it has really been awesome to witness.

Even when mistakes are made he is able to bounce back and learn from his mistakes and not repeat them. That's what a power player does.

A power player isn't perfect, but he or she will admit his or her mistakes and grow from them. Power is all about improvement and growth and being better today than you were yesterday and making a commitment to always strive to be your best.

We talked about mentors, coaches, teachers who help

shape your day to day, but your starting five are your models, the people you aspire to be or who give you the courage to go out and do the things you do. They are the shoulders you stand on to reach your heights.

You can't have a winning team without a solid starting five.

CHAPTER SEVENTEEN

Girl Power

My persuasion can build a nation
Endless power
—Beyoncé, "Run the World (Girls)"

According to the United States Census, women earn seventy-eight cents for every dollar earned by men. The median income for full-time, year-round workers for men is $42,800, compared to $34,700 for women. According to the Bureau of Labor Statistics, one of four women is a chief executive at a company, and when it comes to the Fortune 500 companies, only twenty-four are CEOs. Are there not more women who are qualified? Of course, there are.

But how many women at the top pave the way for others? Or do they see that junior executive as a threat to take her position? Someone to destroy in order to protect her power?

Women make up almost fifty-one percent of the population, so why are there only one hundred or 18.4 percent of women holding the four hundred thirty-five seats in the House of Representatives and there are only twenty women of one hundred in the United States Senate?

While we don't use our political power to send more women to Washington, we certainly have the numbers and power in other areas.

According to MediaPost.com, women account for eighty-five percent of all consumer spending. We could shut down this country if we got together and decided we aren't purchasing this brand or another. Imagine that. But what is power if you don't know how to use it?

Too often, we view another woman's success as somehow holding back our own. That's not just wrong, it's stupid. Just because someone is successful and they happen to be in your field doesn't negate your success. What is for you, is for *you.*

I actually believe that the more you lend a hand, the more hands will be there for you. It's karma. I make it my business to support the women around me who are working toward a goal, big or small.

My niece works for Global Grind as a reporter. At the

premiere for *Beyond the Lights*, she was working the red carpet alongside *People*, *E!*, *Entertainment Weekly*, and the other major media outlets.

The handlers were rushing me through the red carpet to get into the premiere because of time constraints, but I said, "Excuse me, but I have to talk to Global Grind." There was no way I was going in and not give my niece an interview.

After the interview I encouraged her.

"You're amazing," I told her. "I'm so proud of you. Your interview skills are great." She was so gracious and I know she appreciated me saying it.

That's girl power.

When I was working to get a role on *Think Like a Man*, it was actually Will Packer's assistant, Shayla Cowan, who made sure Will looked at my tape. She was the one who urged him to really look at me. And I credit her for being instrumental in me getting the role.

Girl power.

Women don't do enough work grooming one another and working with one another to get ahead. That's why I work so hard in my world to make sure I change that view.

Women need to stop seeing one another as competition, as the enemy, as if there is only one man, one job, one opportunity, and all of us have to scrap over it and kill one another. Why not work together? Why not create more opportunities together?

———————

After *The Love Playbook* came out and was number one on the *New York Times* bestseller list, I was contacted to turn it into a film. I met with several production companies, producers, and directors. Among the dozen or so that I met with, there was one clear choice for me—Queen Latifah.

Queen Latifah is someone I have always admired and we've worked together before on *Single Ladies*, the television show she produced that originally aired on VH1 for three seasons. I played Presley, Omar's big sister. Queen Latifah and I always had a good rapport, but I started thinking, "How powerful would it be to partner with another woman, who I look up to, and work on a movie together?"

There's nothing cooler than girl power and women sticking together. It's something we should see more of. And if I was going to turn my story and my views on love into a film that would empower women, it needed to be powered *by* women. That's how I kept positioning it when I was discussing it with my management team.

"It's so powerful to have two women who are successful coming together," I said. "It's something Hollywood doesn't see a lot."

Why not?

There's so much cattiness with women. We don't support one another the way we should. Instead there is back-biting, backstabbing, and constant put-downs. And that's just in everyday life. You add business or a professional competitiveness to the mix and that negativity gets taken to a whole new level.

I see it all of the time in the entertainment field where you may be competing for the same roles with other women. I totally understand that it's hard to be supportive when you're going for the same role as someone. I'm not saying you go in and say, "Good luck, I hope you do well and get the role." That wouldn't be genuine because, of course, *you* want that spot. But you don't have to be negative and say, "Look at her, she's horrible. I heard [this and that] about her. . . ." Why tear her down? How does that help you? It doesn't. And if she gets the role and you don't, that's no reason to bash her. They may have picked her for a dozen reasons that really had nothing to do with you not being good. Move on. There are other roles, jobs, etc. Keep working on yourself and push to get there. But don't take out another with words or deeds. That will never serve your greater cause, which is to be successful.

I really got to see how deep this thing is with women when I was at the Black Women in Hollywood Luncheon hosted by *Essence* magazine in 2013. Gabrielle Union received an award at that luncheon and during her acceptance speech she stunned the crowd when she shared how she was one of these mean girls. I've known Gabby for quite a while and I had no idea how deep this was for her, and how deep it must be for a lot of women—particularly in our industry.

"We live in a town that rewards pretending and I had been pretending to be fierce and fearless for a very long time," she started. Then she went on to talk about how she used to gossip about other women and lived for the negativity. She said she used to take joy in people's pain and "tap-danced on their misery."

She was that girl. If she wasn't doing well, she didn't want anyone else to be doing well, either.

Gabby wasn't alone. Unfortunately, this attitude is more a rule than the exception.

Many of us at the luncheon that day were surprised by how raw and honest and real Gabrielle was. It was sad and also refreshing that she admitted it. She didn't just tell on herself; she exposed the kind of mean-girl cruelty that is so unfortunately prevalent, and she totally crushed it. Gabby ended her speech with this bit of inspiration:

"Real fierce and fearless women . . . celebrate and compliment other women and we recognize and embrace the notion that their shine in no way diminishes our light, and actually makes our light shine brighter."

When Gabby was through, I was in tears. Most of the women in the audience were crying, too.

It must have been extremely difficult for Gabby to get

up there and tell people that she had been the one making life hell for so many of her sisters in Hollywood. But for her to reevaluate herself and change is one of the biggest power plays a person can make in their lives. Telling the truth about yourself and being willing to honor that truth and then walk a totally new path opens your life to great things.

Look at Gabby's life today: Her career has never been better. She's now starring in a bunch of movies, she has her own one-hour drama on television, and she just got married to NBA great Dwyane Wade.

When you can face your ugliness and change, good things are bound to happen.

Karma.

I've never been one of those women who hated on the success of others. Just the opposite. In Hollywood, there are so few roles for women of color and the same ten actresses invariably end up auditioning for the same ones.

I don't sit in those rooms sizing up each one and tearing them down. Instead, I focus my energy on the things about me that are special. You never have to tear someone down to give yourself an edge.

In addition to telling myself positive things, I also spend a lot of time working on my craft, taking acting lessons, and improving. So when I am in the room it is, "May the best woman win." And if I don't get the job, then it simply wasn't for me, or there's something better waiting for me.

Being negative simply isn't an option for me. Even if bad-mouthing another may work in the short term, eventually you will develop a reputation and you never know when that negativity you put out there will come back to you. Because it always will.

I believe that positivity works the same way.

I was recently at a movie premiere. The performance by the lead actress was so good I needed to let her know. After the screening she was surrounded by press. I waited my turn and I went up to Gugu Mbatha-Raw and told her how amazing she was in *Beyond the Lights.* And how I wished her nothing but success.

She seemed surprised at first. And I get it. Women—particularly women in the same competitive field—rarely compliment and support one another. So your first thought may be, "What's her angle?" But if someone does well at something you should acknowledge it.

I'm sure Gugu heard all night how great she was. But it was important to me that I also let her know. It's cool to empower somebody else. That's where I am at this phase in my life. It's such a powerful thing to pour positivity into someone. Instead of looking at her and saying, "Why did they give *her* the job?" you should know that it was simply *her* opportunity. Your opportunity will come. And if you don't believe that, then perhaps you should pursue other goals.

When a woman rocks, you have to let her know. Hopefully, if Gugu sees my next project she will support it.

Why is it important to support one another? (And really this goes beyond women.) Because I believe that no one gets anywhere on their own. We need one another. Everyone has their own special and unique gifts and by coming together you help someone and help yourself in the process, expanding your opportunities and your world.

What I've always known about women is that if we ever come together we can see some serious changes in this world. That old adage "there's strength in numbers" can apply to us in business and other areas. We have allowed ourselves to not sit in the power seats. Men don't operate like that. Even the most competitive men in the most competitive fields may be ruthless, but when it comes to power and success they know how to work together to make things happen.

I believe women can and must do better.

If you're not used to supporting your sisters, my advice: Practice.

Don't be phony, but when you see another woman genuinely doing a good job at your place of work, let her know.

Try these small but important steps to help boost girl power:

- Stop the judging and negative talk

- Celebrate the achievements of others

- Become a mentor

- Be kind, be respectful

- Support woman-owned businesses and endeavors

People ask me how I can be so positive all of the time. I'd like to say that it really comes with maturity. But truthfully, I've always been this way. I have always been that girl who was supportive of others. But I do know it's hard for some people.

My hairdresser paid me a really nice compliment. She said, "La, when women out here meet you and get to know you they don't even want to fuck your man anymore. They'd rather be your friend."

Now that may have been a crude way of saying that I am a girl's girl. But I got it. And it made me feel good. Because it is the absolute truth. I appreciate that other people understand that about me.

I think in life you can get farther by uplifting and not

hating. Some of my favorite movies are with all-female casts. I celebrate when women work together and find success. I love to see women directors and people like Oprah and Shonda Rhimes making power plays. I pump my fists for them.

When I see them I know that it's possible for a group of dope-ass women to work together and do something fantastic and be successful.

Girl power!

CHAPTER EIGHTEEN

The Power Within

"You've had the power all along, my dear."

A baby has brains, but it doesn't know much. Experience is the only thing that brings knowledge, and the longer you are on earth the more experience you are sure to get.

—L. Frank Baum,
The Wonderful Wizard of Oz

We are all born with everything we need to achieve anything our minds can conceive. At birth. But we need time and experiences to give us the wisdom, knowledge, and courage to go out and get it.

At the end of *The Wizard of Oz*, Glinda the Good Witch floats down from the sky in this pinkish bubble, dressed in her cream-colored taffeta outfit with her wand

and crown. She walks over to Dorothy, who is clutching Toto close to her chest.

Dorothy says in a panic, "Will you help me? Can you help me?"

Glinda smiles and says, "You don't need to be helped any longer. You've always had the power to go back to Kansas."

The scarecrow asks Glinda why she didn't tell Dorothy before.

"Because she wouldn't have believed me," said Glinda. "She had to learn it for herself."

The Alchemist by Paulo Coelho talks about the very same thing. In the story the wanderer traveled many lands searching for this one thing that he was told would change his existence only to discover that what he traveled for through the desert, through danger, defeating death was right where he started all along. It was literally in his backyard.

I definitely relate to looking inside yourself for your power. I also see the message Glinda delivered to Dorothy another way as well. A lot of times people never reach their potential or pursue their dreams because they allow outside factors to hold them back. It's easy to find blame in your circumstances.

"My dad was never around" or "I come from a messed-up family" or "I'm just doing what I was taught in my home . . ."

People have a bunch of excuses for why they aren't good at something or aren't successful. But the truth is it comes down to that person. You do have the power within to accomplish anything. But you have to believe it.

Just because your father wasn't there for you, doesn't stop you. And that doesn't mean that you can't be there for your children. You have the power to be a good parent. If you come from a messed-up or dysfunctional family, you have the power to change the course of how you grow up. You can change your destiny.

It doesn't matter how poor you were, if you had a bad education, if you didn't feel loved. Whatever the case, you may have been dealt a bad hand, but how you play it is up to you. If you feel as though you don't have enough knowledge, start reading. Famed playwright August Wilson (*Fences, The Piano Lesson, Two Trains Running*) dropped out of high school in the tenth grade. But he didn't let that stop him. He spent his days in the library reading everything he could get his hands on. He got his G.E.D. and went on to win several Tonys and two Pulitzer Prizes for Drama.

You have to find out what you're made of. You must tap into your inner power—you need to know whether you *can* accomplish and complete your goals. Push yourself and see who you really are.

As I mentioned earlier, I went to the screening of *Beyond the Lights*, It was about a girl who becomes a pop star.

She was very successful, but she tried to kill herself. I could hear the people in the theater saying, "Her life was popping, why would she want to kill herself?"

I know people in real life who are rich and successful who are miserable. They are pursuing external, material, and superficial things and not working or building themselves or what's inside.

I have two friends who recently celebrated their fifteenth wedding anniversary. I love being around them because you can just see how much they still love each other. I asked Nadia how she and her husband were going to celebrate.

"We're going to our favorite spot—Joe's Crab Shack," she said.

They didn't need to go to the south of France or some Caribbean island or do something exotic to celebrate their love. They were doing something that they both enjoyed— eat seafood—and it was real simple. It would be cool to go to Baskin-Robbins and share an ice-cream cone. It's the love of what you two share, not what you do, that's so powerful.

In work and business, people get this twisted, too. It's the pursuit of the thing that feeds your soul, not the results—the money and the things—that should matter.

The journey to discover what it is you're really about is what should matter. And at each stage, you should stop and take stock and not try to rush through the process to get to where you want to go. Because each stage matters.

I learned so much working as an intern at the radio station that prepared me for what I'm doing today. I learned the business from the ground up. I learned how to conduct myself from watching how people did it right and how people did it wrong. I learned humility and the power of serving others. I learned that hard work could lead to opportunities as I went from being an intern to an on-air jock. I watched what happens when you play your position and network. I watched others around me, like Ludacris, take risks and follow their dreams and win.

None of those lessons would have happened if I felt at any time I was too good to be an intern or didn't take the job seriously.

And in doing those early jobs and taking chances along the way—like heading off to Los Angeles without knowing a single soul—you learn who you are. Like Dorothy in *The Wizard of Oz*, your adventures along that road reveal your character and eventually will lead you to where you need to be.

The biggest power play in the world is understanding your own power and then unleashing it to reach your goals and follow your dreams.

ACKNOWLEDGMENTS

Thank you, GOD, for never leaving my side.

I've been so blessed to have the best family and friends in my corner. Life is so much easier because of all of you.

To my business team: Know that I appreciate each and every one of you. I can't do this alone.

Love always.